Library of Congress Cataloging-in-Publication Data

Fields, Wilmer, My Life in the Negro Leagues: An Autobiography, with a forward by John B. Holway

Baseball, Negro Leagues, sports history

Summary: Negro Leagues player Wilmer Fields tells the story of playing baseball before professional sports was integrated.

E-ISBN: 978-1-939282-08-8

Published by Miniver Press, LLC, McLean Virginia

Copyright 2013 Wilmer Fields, Jr.

All rights reserved under International and Pan-American Copyright Conventions. By payment of the required fees, you have been granted the non-exclusive, non-transferable right to access and read the text of this e-book on-screen. No part of this text may be reproduced, transmitted, down-loaded, decompiled, reverse engineered, or stored in or introduced into any information storage and retrieval system, in any form or by any means, whether electronic or mechanical, now known or hereinafter invented, without the express written permission of Nell Minow. For information regarding permission, write to editor@miniverpress.com

Re-issued with a new introduction June 2013

Wilmer Fields

My Life in the Negro Leagues

My Life in the Negro Leagues

An Autobiography by

Wilmer Fields

**With a Foreword
By John B. Holway**

Miniver Press

A limited number of copies of the first edition of this book are available for $30 unsigned or $100 signed by Wilmer Fields, authenticated by his son. For more information or to place an order, email **bfmanassas@aol.com**

*To my wife Audrey,
our children Marvin, Maridel, and Wilmer, Jr.,
our loved ones, and fans of
the Black Legends of Baseball*

Contents

Foreword ix
Introduction xiii

1. Pursuing a Dream 1
2. Whole New World 5
3. The Homestead Grays 9
4. The Grays—Excellence on the Field 17
5. Time Out for War 27
6. Saying No to the Majors 31
7. North of the Border 39
8. The End of the Road 59
9. Lessons Learned 61
10. Better Late than Never 67
11. Everything Starts with Family 75
12. Looking Back 81

Appendix 85
Index 89

Foreword

Wilmer "Red" Fields is a big, hearty, bubbly man with a broad smile and a merry laugh.

He's also a walking history book of the old Negro Leagues of the 1940s. His vivid stories of America of 40–50 years ago breathe life into the dusty newspaper files that historians usually wander through.

I first met Wilmer in the winter of 1969 when I published an article on Josh Gibson in the Washington *Post*. That morning his wife, Audrey, called to say her husband had played with Josh—and that both of us lived in the very same town, Manassas, Virginia. I tell this as an example of how primitive Negro League research was at that time.

What a treasure! Wilmer and I have spent hour upon hour sitting in his den listening to him spin stories of Satchel Paige, Buck Leonard, and the other immortals of black baseball—men who have indeed been made immortal, thanks to Fields' vibrant memories of those summers of long ago.

We've gone to radio interviews together, baseball fan meetings together, and cookouts together. (At one of the latter, I challenged him to a ping pong game, which he won 21–1.)

Wilmer's son Billy starred in basketball in high school in Manassas, in college at Providence, and in the pro leagues in Europe.

In the heyday of his own baseball career, the senior Fields was a double-threat man, starring in the pitcher's box and at bat.

"Red Fields had a lot of nerve," former shortstop Tom "Pee Wee" Butts of the Baltimore Elite Giants told me. "Most pitchers can't come back when you get three or four hits off them, but he could. Most fellows get shaky and blow up, but it looked like he came back with more. That's what I call hanging in there. Had a chance to win his own game at bat too."

Like most pitchers, Fields was proud of his hitting—with good reason. In Latin America he led the league at bat several times against competition that included major leaguers such as Brooks Robinson, Lou Burdette, Larry Doby, and others.

He likes to recall batting against Satchel Paige in Puerto Rico. Fields smacked a two-run homer against a local pitcher, and later Satchel was brought in to relieve. He whiffed the New York Giants' Les Layton on three fastballs at the knees.

"I was next up," Fields says. We knew each other from the Negro Leagues, so I got the lightest bat I could find. He threw me a fast one, and I missed it."

"Aw, you can't hit," Paige taunted him.

"But I knew he was going to throw the same pitch, and I hit it out of there." As Wilmer rounded third, he called to Satch, "Old man, go back home."

As he crossed home plate and turned toward the dugout, the Latin fans thrust bills through the chicken wire fence in front of the stands. "One guy gave me $100," Fields recalls. "I never will forget it."

"Most pitchers on the Grays were good hitters," recalled Vic Harris, Fields' first manager. "When we put Fields on third base, he was as good as any third baseman we had fielding."

Wilmer is so light-skinned that Ted "Double Duty" Radcliffe laughingly calls him "the man who integrated the Homestead Grays."

Fields got the assignment of going into restaurants to order hamburgers for the team, his hat pulled down low. When the disguise didn't work, he was often summarily ordered out. "I thought it was funny at the time," he chuckles. "I still do."

They ate what they could, where they could. Sometimes they played a double-header on two hot dogs. "And one time in Newark we got ahold of some bad hot dogs."

They traveled by bus, harmonizing or playing cards as the miles rolled by. "It was very seldom for a whole lot of money. Back in those days there wasn't a whole lot of money." When the driver got sleepy, one of the players was roused out of sleep to take over for him. "We're just lucky we never had any bad accidents, I guess."

The fun-loving Josh Gibson put the rookie up to some of his mischief. When the bus rolled through the mountain tunnels on the Pennsylvania Turnpike, Josh nudged Wilmer, who let out a shout, as the sound reverberated off the walls and the startled players jumped awake.

Fields' main rival on the Grays was 6'7" pitcher Garnet Blair, an old college rival in both baseball and basketball. Each tried to best the other. Chuckled Harris: "If Fields won his game, Blair was going to try to win his, going to out-pitch Fields, and vice versa." While Harris gleefully watched the competition, the only ones who weren't gleeful were the Grays' opponents.

Wilmer lost three big seasons, ages 20–23, to World War II.

When he returned in 1946, he enjoyed the best season of his career. His best game that year was his last, an exhibition against Johnny "Double No-Hit" Vander Meer of the Cincinnati Reds.

"I think Vander Meer struck out 12, and I struck out 11. He allowed three hits. I allowed four. He had control, good control, like throwing darts. Didn't look like his curve was that big, but he threw it where he wanted it."

Reds catcher Ray Meuller caught Vandy. "I knew he wouldn't guess curve and take a chance on getting hit by a fastball, so I just threw him curves all day long."

The final score was Vander Meer 1, Fields 0.

The next spring Jackie Robinson stepped onto the field in a Dodger uniform, and the Negro Leagues began their steep demise. In 1948 Fields pitched in the last great black World Series, against the Birmingham Black Barons and their rookie outfielder, Willie Mays.

"Mays got one hit the whole Series," Fields says, "a curve ball that hung up in his eyes that [Grays pitcher] R. T. Walker threw. They wouldn't even send him out there against me."

Wilmer pitched his game in New Orleans after a 25-hour car ride from Washington. He arrived shaking from the grueling drive.

"I was in such bad shape out there, the fastball wouldn't go straight, it would run the other way. I never threw a running fastball before in my life." The Barons were so surprised that "there wasn't anything to it. The final score was 14–1, if I'm not mistaken. [Grays first baseman] Luke Easter hit a homer or a triple. That's when Cleveland grabbed him."

The Grays won the Series in five games.

Could Fields have joined Easter and Mays in the major leagues? "I knew I could have made it in the majors," he says. "No doubt in my mind at all." But he was making too much money in the black leagues, Canada, and Latin America.

Now a retired counselor of alcoholics, Fields is in demand as a speaker about the Negro Leagues. I watched him talk to sixth-grade students at one local school, explaining about a world of segregation that neither they nor their parents had ever experienced. Their questions tended to cover the same ground as they grappled to comprehend what he was trying to tell them.

Then he patiently signed autographs for a line of kids that never seemed to grow shorter. When the bell rang, the line still stretched out into the hall. So Wilmer took all their scraps of paper home and signed several dozen more, which he mailed back to the kids who hadn't gotten one.

His greatest thrill came in 1958 at the end of his career in Mexico City. "Have you ever been to that park?" he asked me. "If you ever have a chance, look at dead center field, where they have a scoreboard. I hit one past that scoreboard, must have gone 525 feet, the only one had ever been hit out there, and Mays and all of them had been there.

"The night before, this boy threw me a curve ball, and I hit it on the handle, and I'm a pretty good curve ball hitter. So the next day he came in to relieve, and I got a 37-ounce bat—I use a heavier bat against curve ball pitchers. He threw the same pitch, and I swung.

"I wish you had seen that one."

So do I.

John B. Holway

Introduction

This book was written so that the public will know about the black baseball players of the Negro Leagues during the 1930s, 1940s, and 1950s.

It will also explain why one black baseball player, who played 25 years of professional baseball, preferred to play in the Negro Leagues and foreign countries rather than accept any of five major league contracts that were offered to him.

As a child, my dream was to be a part of black baseball. Back then, black children had limited access to sports. We had to try and satisfy our needs in any way we could afford. We took advantage of every opportunity we had, and black baseball was one.

Black baseball allowed a black country boy to live a dream come true. That is why my love for black baseball is so strong, and why I hope this book will keep it alive.

1

Pursuing a Dream

I was born in the small country town of Manassas, Virginia, in 1922. I became interested in baseball as soon as I found out what it was. When I was old enough to pick up a piece of wood and use it as a bat, I started hitting rocks. Sometimes I'd hit rocks for 30 minutes or longer. Hit 'em until my hands got sore and I couldn't hit 'em anymore. Other times, I'd throw rubber balls against the house. I'd try to improve on every pitch, aiming to hit a certain spot. There were times when a broken window resulted, but my parents overlooked these mishaps most of the time.

I can remember playing baseball games with my family on Sundays before church. I was eight years old. We played our games in the front yard and our mother would always remind us to watch out for her flowers. We had a lot of fun.

As I look back on that wholesome life, I see that love and caring meant more to us than anything. The goodness and discipline we received from our parents has lasted. Sometimes, it's hard to believe that things have changed so much in society.

Our family included our mother and father, Albert and Mabel Fields, and the children: Evelyn, Morris, Marvin, Oliver, and myself. Our love for each other was very strong, and we treasured our values. I wish I could have played some of the sports that are available to children today. We didn't have so much, but we appreciated what we did have.

There was a large field in front of our house. All the neighbors and a few outsiders would play a game of baseball there every day. The bats would be a stick or board, and the ball would be a roll of rags. We had so much fun that it didn't matter to us what we played with. That kind of fun doesn't exist today. We always had plenty of food and a place to call home. Again, the love and caring in our home was very strong, and that's what made everything all right.

Our parents gave us the opportunity to go to college. On a minimum salary they were able to provide us with the necessities of life. The love and religion that were practiced in our home have been passed on to our children and grandchildren. It's the backbone of our family.

During my early childhood years I enjoyed helping my father on our small farm. My everyday duties included feeding the animals and bringing in wood. My father would give me 25 cents per week. I'd also help my mother inside the house. Then there were the times when dad would let me drive the horse and buggy two miles to go fishing. One day while I was fishing, I was looking at the water and I felt something rolling under my feet. I glanced down and there was a six-foot snake! I jumped straight up in the air about two feet. That snake scared me so bad I was shaking, so I got a stick just in case it came back.

I remember when my brother Oliver and I used to battle each other in horseshoe games. We didn't have regular horseshoes, so our father would give us the worn ones off his horses. Sometimes, if we got a well-balanced one, we would flip a penny for it. Our father and our friends would join in on the fun. I really enjoyed my childhood.

I remember the days when I would be walking down the dusty road from school and I'd be thinking about some day playing baseball as a professional. My favorite team was the New York Yankees, and my favorite players were Babe Ruth, Lou Gehrig, and Lefty Gomez. Those days, no one thought of black baseball players going into the major leagues. But, when I said my prayers, I asked the Lord to give me the physical ability and talent so that I could some day play professional baseball.

I often wondered what it would take for a black person to play professional baseball. As I grew older, I found out that there were some black baseball teams in the Washington, D.C. area. Because of segregation, the black children in Manassas were restricted from playing in many of the activities in the area. That led me to believe that there was no way a black person would play in the major leagues.

When I was 13 years old, I would read about black baseball teams and players in the black newspapers that were sold in D.C. and Richmond. When I read about the large number of spectators that attended black baseball games at Griffith Stadium in Washington, I became even more interested in hearing and learning more about the black leagues.

In high school we played only three or four games a year. Our uniforms, equipment, and playing conditions were poor. But when I was 16 years old, I was influenced by some of the older Manassas baseball players to play for the town team. There were other boys my age on the team. Sandlot baseball in Manassas was a Sunday and holiday affair. My father used to love to come to the games and talk to his friends while we played. He was a loyal and dedicated fan of all of his sons' baseball careers.

When the Manassas sandlot team disbanded before my senior year of high school, a team in Fairfax, Virginia asked my brothers and me to join them, and we did. Hitting home runs in Fairfax was somewhat easy because it had a small playing field. I was 16 years old, and I was throwing the ball pretty well. When I turned 17, some of the Fairfax team management asked me if I'd be interested in trying out for the Homestead Grays. At that time, the Grays were the best black team in America!

At last, my prayers were answered; the prayers I had prayed so long. I guess I was more shocked than anything to get the chance to play professional baseball for the greatest black team in the world. Some people doubted I could make it. I remember at my high school graduation, one student gave me some phony money to get back home after I didn't make it. It was supposed to be a joke, but I took it as a challenge instead. Sometimes an inappropriate remark can motivate a person to try harder. That one motivated me.

I got the opportunity to pitch for Homestead against a semi-pro team in Ballston, Virginia. I was unfamiliar with professional baseball and I made some mistakes during the game. But I got my first professional win, and the Grays offered me a contract. I was 17 years old. What a great feeling!

When I left home in 1939 to play baseball with the Grays, my mother gave me a Bible to take with me. I read this Bible every day and it gave me strength and faith. I even played baseball with that Bible. I'd wrap it up in a sock and stick it in my pants pocket. That same Bible sits on my table at home, and that same faith exists within me today.

2

Whole New World

Leaving home at 17 was an experience I'll never forget. The day I reported to the Grays was a nightmare. They were staying at the Logan Hotel in Washington, and no player even so much as spoke to me for two hours. I guess they thought I was a custodian. My peg pants didn't help the situation any. When we got on the bus to go to the field, they told me to sit on the back seat. It didn't bother me because that's where I'd been sitting on buses my whole life! But that's where the sweaty uniforms hung sometimes, and this often made it difficult to breathe. When the condition was too bad, I'd go to the front of the bus and sit on the steps next to the driver.

Being from a small town and totally inexperienced for what might happen in a big city was like going into a battle. When the older players spoke I listened. We had 17 players on the 1939 team, and the closest teammate in age to me was 26 years old. Some of the older players had as much as 20 years experience in professional baseball. My parents taught me to listen, and that is what I did. No one hollered at me because they knew I was a young country boy that hadn't been exposed to the life of a professional.

Trying to get involved in a conversation with the Grays was very hard. Even though I was being laughed at and ridiculed, it didn't bother me because I was determined to stay with Homestead. No one told me anything as I warmed up before a game. The isolation was like being in a country where no one spoke English but me. The only thing I received from the manager, Vic Harris, was the baseball, what he called "that little white pill." I wasn't about to ask any ridiculous questions, so I just went out and gave the best effort I could, and observed the veterans to see what they were doing.

When we played in small ballparks I felt more secure because I was accustomed to playing before small crowds. There was less chance of being booed and better opportunities to become involved in the game. You see, the Grays didn't think I was ready for major league competition, and I agreed because my experience was limited at that time.

Meal money was $1.25 a day in 1939. Being from a family where food was always available, this meant quite an adjustment. My eating habits turned to junk food. Hot dogs and hamburgers made up my daily menu, with french apple pie, meringue pie, and milk for dessert. But there were times that I treated myself to a wholesome meal. I think I was trying to find my mother's cooking.

One of my duties as a rookie with Homestead was to watch the luggage on top of our bus during a ballgame. After the game it was back to the bus, and on to the next city. Sometimes I ran errands for the ballplayers. I did this to show my appreciation for the help I received from them. My teammates would do things like offer me food. I was trying very hard to succeed in every aspect of the game, and I wanted to be accepted as an intricate part of their operation. So the support I received from the Grays made me feel as if I was at home in my mother's kitchen.

Since I was from the country, my teammates had to do things like remind me to stop shaking on the mound when I pitched against a white team. One of the hardest adjustments I had to make was to stop looking at the scoreboard while I was pitching. I was interested in the inning and I'd wonder if I'd be able to finish the game. That habit stayed with me a few years.

The Grays picked their spots for me to pitch early on. They never threw me to the wolves or disgraced me in any fashion. Sometimes they'd let me pitch against a Negro American League team in an exhibition game (Homestead was in the Negro National League), but when we went to Yankee Stadium or some other major league park, my duties were limited.

When coming home after the season ended in 1939, I was trying to meet my brothers one day to play a game on their team. I was real tired when I boarded the train in Washington, and when the train hit Manassas, I was asleep. The conductor's hollering at the Nokesville, Virginia station, about eight miles past Manassas, woke me up. I was determined to play with my brothers that day, so I ran to the opening between the passenger cars, threw my two paper suitcases off first, and jumped. The train was traveling somewhat slow through the Nokesville crossing, but the step of the train hit me in the buttocks and knocked me about 10 feet. I have never been hit that hard in my life! My hip gives me trouble to this day. Luckily, a man picked me up and drove me home for two dollars, and although I wanted to play one more time with my brothers, it just wasn't meant to be.

Through football and studies I was able to acquire a football scholarship to Virginia State College. During my senior year in high school, my grades were good. Reverend Barnes, the school principal, talked to me about my grade point average for four years. He told me I had a 3.2 on a four-point scale. Boy, was I surprised!

Anyway, the football program at Manassas Industrial School was the strongest sport. I was selected from our small school to an All-Conference football team that included players from D.C., Virginia, Maryland, and Delaware. It was an honor for me. I broke my leg playing football, and that, too, has plagued me my whole life. The conference that Virginia State belonged to said I wasn't allowed to play conference games because I had played professional sports. So my freshman year was centered around playing against freshman teams from other colleges. Fortunately they changed the rule in time for my second year.

One of the most inspiring moments of my early baseball career came one day at college. I was returning from the dining room when the mailman handed me a box. I always received boxes from my mother, but never from anyone else. Especially anyone from Pittsburgh, Pennsylvania, where this box was postmarked. I opened the box in the middle of campus because my friends thought it was food, and inside was a baseball-shaped radio that was 10 inches across. At the bottom of the radio was an inscription that read: National Negro World Champions 1940. All of my friends admired the radio, especially my roommate, Lawrence "Old Gal" Lewis. He wouldn't let anyone hold it. I also have a 1940 World Champion jacket. After my first year with the Grays, it suddenly felt urgent to think about playing professional baseball as a livelihood.

3

The Homestead Grays

The city of Homestead, Pennsylvania was the home of the Grays. It's a small town located across the river from Pittsburgh. In the 1930s and 1940s, it was a manufacturing town. Residents of the city had to go to Pittsburgh for recreation of any kind. The factories operated 24 hours a day. All of the houses or establishments were black or brown from smoke. The restaurants were small but their chili and pies were always tempting. I could walk down the hill to eat breakfast and have to change my shirt within two hours because of the smoke. The meeting place for sports people was "The Sky Rocket." This establishment was owned by "Sonny Man" Jackson; he also owned the Grays in the 1940s. When we left Homestead for a road trip, the people would gather around the bus to wish us well. It was a small city, and everyone respected each other, regardless of color.

Joining the Grays at such a young age, and trying to see my place on the best black team in America, was a puzzle to me. I didn't know where I'd fit at first, but as time went by, I learned by trial and error. My knowledge of professional baseball increased rapidly. Through long years of hard work, I was able to put this knowledge into action. When you love a sport as much as I loved baseball, you learn to accept mistakes and profit from them. I was willing to take my bumps and knocks along the way—after all, I was a country boy and a rookie. Having a desire to make it in your life-dream means taking on all enemies so that you can succeed.

There was no playing around in the dugout of the Homestead Grays. Players such as Buck Leonard and Sam Bankhead saw to that. No one was allowed in the dugout during a game. Photographers were shooed away before a game. We were a bunch of dedicated employees. I can sincerely say that I was brought up the right way both at home and then with the Grays.

We conducted ourselves off the field in the same way we did on it: like professionals. At no time, that I can remember, did a Homestead Gray become incarcerated. The organization would not stand for that kind of negative publicity. Therefore, the ballplayers represented the Grays like professionals. In fact, I can't ever remember a player even being punished for negative behavior.

Our reputation carried us to such heights that the public demanded certain characteristics from Negro League ballplayers. To give you an idea of how the Grays' reputation preceded them, one time we were playing a team from Brunswick, N.Y. (a section of New York that rooted for the Brooklyn Dodgers). Anyway, a disagreement occurred between the two managers and the umpires over back-to-back Homestead home runs that were disputed. The fans booed the Brunswick team.

Then there was the time a boy from Brooklyn was our batboy. After a game his mother confronted the Grays over the amount of money her son was paid. The Gray's secretary gave the boy additional money, but the mother wasn't satisfied. She said, "You should be ashamed of yourselves for giving my son so little money." Now the secretary had a good idea of what batboys earned, but it seems this mother had heard about the Homestead Grays' wealth.

The only incident I can remember occurring in Griffith Stadium involved the Grays and the Atlanta Black Crackers from the Southern League. The umpire made a call at home plate and the Crackers' management argued. The incident became so inflamed that the Crackers' ballplayer hit the umpire. But that was the only time I can remember a problem at Griffith Stadium.

If we arrived at a ballpark early, the club would take extra hitting and fielding practice. We took advantage of any time we'd get. This was a time the players really enjoyed. It gave us the opportunity to play other positions, and it gave the pitchers the chance to show our ability as hitters. We'd bet a Coca-Cola on who would hit one out of the park first.

The Grays had a complete team. The pitching staff consisted of Ray Brown, Roy Welmaker, Johnny Wright, Roy Partlow, Garnet Blair, Bill Pope, Edsel Walker, "Groundhog" Thompson, and myself. But the strongest point of the team was our offense. Being surrounded by quality ballplayers enabled me to get better through knowledge and experience. As time passed, my acquisition of baseball skills became a reality. When I wasn't pitching for the Grays, I was always trying my hand at other positions in practice. The ability to play other positions became important over the years because the managers, Vic Harris and Sam Bankhead, would ask me to perform various duties besides pitching. I looked at the great ones around me for inspiration in those cases, especially the One upstairs. This willingness to learn paid off in the future because the New York Yankees wanted me to play third base, the Brooklyn Dodgers wanted me as a pitcher, and the Detroit Tigers organization wanted me as an outfielder. There were other major league clubs that wanted my services as well.

I believe that being able to do more than one thing in life makes one's life more secure. Finding more than one way to accomplish any part of your life is an asset. If an individual is sincere in his or her endeavors, determination will overcome the obstacles of life. For instance, in the 1930s and 1940s, there was very little in the way of sports for black people. Therefore, making a living in black baseball was a rarity. Life could be a struggle at times, but it was a happy one!

Life on the road was often inconvenient. For example, if the Grays played in a small city, the facilities also would be small. So small, in fact, that not all the players could get dressed in the locker room at the same time. So when the game was in the seventh inning, the manager would let some of the team go and dress, and the rest of us would change after the game. Another inconvenience was a shortage of water—hot water, that is. The last players in to shower went without. At major league parks there was plenty of room and we really appreciated that. But even when there were inconveniences, I never saw a sign of resentment from the players. We knew that eventually we'd be going back to the hotel or a house, and then we'd get relief.

Staying at the homes of families in the towns where we played was nice. There was a clean atmosphere, but the inconvenience the families had to endure was noticeable. Most of the time we stayed in black hotels or houses. In some cities, like New York, there were better hotels for us to stay in but because we were financially limited we stayed at a place where the club booked us. Obviously, there were few hotels down South available to us, and these were often very rundown, so we stayed mostly in homes. The team would be scattered with ballplayers in different homes. It was inconvenient at times, like when it was time for the club to go to the ballpark, or to a restaurant, or to leave the city. It was rare that anyone got left in a town, but it did happen.

After the team had been on the road for awhile, a bed of any kind looked like paradise. I stayed in a Y.M.C.A. one time when I was with the Indianapolis Clowns. Sometimes you don't know how well off you are in life until you go through a change in status. If you were a youngster trying to make it in the Negro Leagues in the 1930s and 1940s, you didn't complain about anything at any time. You had to be able to ride in a bus all night, and then go out and produce on the field the next day. That was a must. Being able to deal within that structure was a big part of whether or not you would mature into a good ballplayer. The older members of the team set examples of how things were done, and then the younger ballplayers were expected to follow them. No excuses.

People often don't believe me when I tell them about some of the things we had to go through when I played ball. Like being escorted from the field by policemen after things got out of hand. Spectators would bet on what every ballplayer would do in a game, and if you didn't meet their expectations you would sometimes be abused. When we'd arrive at a ballpark we'd have to enter by the gate in center field. We weren't allowed to go into the park through the front gate where the home team entered. Our manager would complain to the other team's manager and he'd promise it wouldn't ever happen again. Sometimes when I look back, it's hard to believe some of the horrible things we had to endure. But that was the way it was in the 1930s, 1940s, and 1950s.

The Homestead Grays traveled more than any other team in the Negro National League. Because of their popularity, the Grays were in demand all over the country on a regular basis. Traveling 500 miles after playing a double header was routine. We would leave Pittsburgh, then drive to Buffalo just to play one night game. Then we would return home and play in Pittsburgh the next night. Or we'd play a double header at Griffith Stadium in Washington, D.C. on Sunday, then leave for St. Louis and play two more games there on Tuesday night.

One time our bus was in a garage being fixed, so we had to travel by cars to play a game about 100 miles from Pittsburgh. When the Grays arrived at the ballpark, we found out the game was cancelled because of the rainy conditions that day. So we head back to Homestead, but on the way, one of the cars hydroplaned and flipped over. In it was "Lick" Carlisle and Boojum Wilson. Carlisle weighed 155 pounds soaking wet, and Wilson a beefy 200 pounds with a size 7½ hat. After the accident, everyone regained their composure when we saw they were alright, but, somehow, during the accident, Wilson's hat got on Lick's head and it was so big it covered his eyes. So the accident brought a scare and more than a few laughs of relief.

I remember when it rained a couple of days in a row when I was playing for Homestead. This gave the ballplayers an unusual chance to enjoy some free time. We would shoot pool, or go to the movies or the circus in Pittsburgh. Some of the ballplayers used to say, "The Lord knows how much we can take," when they were enjoying the rainy day off. But the owners would be disappointed and show it by having sad faces when a game would get rained out.

There is very little traveling today compared to back then. Very little of the toughness of the old days remains. Everything these days is peaches and cream. No one knows how good a black ballplayer back then would have been if he had received the treatment that ballplayers receive today. Somebody had to pay the price (of segregation) and we were the unfortunate ones.

The hot summers brought out the uncomfortable side of that life. We didn't have any air conditioning on the bus or in some of the places we stayed. But regardless of how hot it would get, no one would complain, and no one was indecent. Someone might take off his shirt while traveling since it would get soaked with sweat. But our uniforms would dry rapidly when we hung them in the back of the bus. If we arrived at the ballpark early, we'd lay our still-wet uniforms on the grass and let them finish drying there.

The togetherness and family atmosphere on the Grays helped make things more comfortable. We had two quartets on our bus, and we sang spirituals and Mills Brothers songs. One group was very good, and the other was very bad. I sang with a group called The Impossibles. We sang because it carried us back to our homelife, and it gave us a way to relax.

The Grays were a very close-knit team. If you saw one Gray, there were bound to be others nearby. After all, we depended on each other for everything. To make sure we were on time for the bus, to share food from under our seats, to share equipment if a teammate forgot his, and so on.

We even shared soap and shoe shine polish. We'd switch seats on the bus so that our trips were more comfortable.

Our closeness carried us through many trials and tribulations.

One of the things I enjoyed while we traveled was looking at the growth of the different crops and plants we'd pass along the way. I would compare them with my father's produce back home and wonder which was the best. But then we'd enter a city and any thoughts of the nature scenes would be quickly erased. Sometimes we'd stop at a roadside market to buy fruit. Fruit in those days was good—not sprinkled with chemical solutions to maintain its color like nowadays.

We traveled with our luggage on top of the bus, so when it rained, of course, our bags would get wet and we'd have to move them. Our driver was always taking shortcuts to try and make up for lost time. To break the tension that would sometimes build up on the bus, we would throw empty bottles at telephone poles while moving at about 55 miles per hour. Sometimes, when we were traveling in the South at night, we'd have to stop for gas. Usually, gas stations were combined with a general store. When the bus driver stopped by the gas pump we made sure he had a large bill so he could go in the store and get change. Once in the store he would order food for us. If the driver had entered the store just to buy food, he would have been told to get out. We had less trouble traveling by night. We used to stop at state parks and drink water from the springs and pumps located there. That was always a pleasure.

When we traveled 100 miles or less we felt relieved. If it was a long trip, sometimes we'd relieve the driver to give him a rest. It was always hard to sleep on the bus because it vibrated so much. The only disagreement between two players on the Grays that I saw in my 11 years with them came while traveling. We accepted traveling as a means to an end, and we put up with it because we wanted to play baseball in the worst way. We rode on a bus that was painted with the words "Blue Goose" on both sides, and it gave people a good impression as we traveled.

During the 1930s and 1940s, fans really enjoyed black baseball. The Washington Senators would draw 7,500 fans to Griffith Stadium for their game, and then the Grays would come into town and bring in up to 20,000! Most of the fans were black, although we had white fans in attendance. I think the black fans came to the stadium to put all their worries behind them. They were such good fans that they would even applaud a good play in practice. Griffith Stadium was one of my favorite places to play. I lost only one game while pitching there, and I think my success there tended to relax me more than at some other ballparks.

It was a joy to autograph pictures and cards for children—most of whom were black. These autograph seekers would arrive well before game time accompanied by their parents. Most of our fans came as families, which made our games a family affair. They would make going to a game a family day. When I look at pictures from back then, it reminds me of the good old days of black baseball.

4

The Grays—Excellence on the Field

It's hard to say how many black ballplayers from the National and American Negro Leagues in the 1930s, 1940s and 1950s would have played in the major leagues had it not been for segregation. It is my opinion that many members of the Grays could have played major league baseball. I base my opinion on 25 years of playing against all different levels of players, including major leaguers, and I think my experience gives me the proper authority to make that judgment. During the peak of the Grays' existence, there was no doubt that their ballplayers were capable of playing major league baseball if they had been given the chance. Forty years after their heyday, people in baseball still recognize the ability of black ballplayers of that era. There were black ballplayers in the Negro Leagues that were average at best, but when they joined the major leagues they became stars.

And there is no question that these men would have succeeded with today's treatments and technology. The black ballplayers of yesteryear succeeded in spite of many hardships they had to overcome: poor travel arrangements, poor eating habits, prejudice, etc. So if we had received the benefits of today's players, there's no telling how good we could have been.

Unfortunately, we will never know statistically just how good many of these players were because very few records were kept on black baseball players during the 1930s and 1940s. And if something was written about a black ballplayer, it was usually about a longtime player. At no time in my baseball career in the States can I remember ever seeing an advertisement with my name on it. The club didn't want to invest any money in advertising. In 1946, the year I had a 16–1 record, I thought I would get some recognition, but I didn't.

Because of the poor recordkeeping of black players, the Homestead players kept their own record of all the strengths and weaknesses of every opponent in the Negro National League, and some in the American League too. Sometimes this information would come from a player who had played in Latin America and had learned about another player there.

In the black leagues, each team had three or four good pitchers. These pitchers would start when we played in major league parks. We would play there when the major league teams were on the road. Or we would throw our best pitchers whenever we expected a big crowd. During my early years with the Grays, teams were intimidated when they played us. I remember one opposing ballplayer who came up to me and asked me not to pitch against his team one night. He said they had been traveling all day and night. The Grays would play a team 20 times and lose only two at the most. The pitching staff was extremely competitive, and each pitcher tried to outdo the others. That made it hard on our opponents! But, more important, it established a pitcher's reputation as one to be used in big games.

Homestead had a tradition of playing in a major league ballpark on holidays. The owners enjoyed these arrangements because it meant a big payday was imminent. You would always see the owners around the ballpark on a holiday. We'd play a double header on these holidays, and the good pitchers would be rested in order to pitch on those occasions. Even though I would have only one or two days' rest, the managers never hesitated to give me the ball. This happened to me not only with the Grays, but in Latin American countries and Canada as well. I can't remember a manager ever asking me how I felt, either. They knew I'd give 100 percent. In fact, one time I pitched a complete game at Griffith Stadium on a Sunday, pitched three innings of relief against the Baltimore Elite Giants on Monday, and then turned around and pitched again on Wednesday. I was sitting in the dugout at Forbes Field in Pittsburgh before the game on Wednesday, and Vic Harris, the manager, gave me the ball again. I looked somewhat befuddled because some of the other pitchers on the team hadn't pitched in a week. The game was being played in honor of Cum Posey—a former owner of the Grays—and Harris wanted me to pitch. I managed to survive nine innings and win, but when the game was over it dawned on me the significance of being asked to pitch. It was an honor to be given the ball on such an important occasion.

During my years with the Grays, I came to find out that we were respected so much that any team that beat us felt they had accomplished the unusual. A good example of this came from former major leaguer Sammy Jethroe, who had played for the Cleveland Buckeyes in the Negro Leagues before switching over. Twenty years after the fact, Jethroe was still bragging about the Buckeyes beating the Grays in the 1945 World Series.

Playing for the Grays gave me a feeling of security. I always felt that the good would overcome the bad when I was with them. There was a feeling of belief surrounding the team that nothing was impossible. The Grays would turn it up a notch whenever a situation required it. The Grays always believed that they deserved the respect they got from other teams. The Grays established a record in the Negro National League that no other team in the league came close to. That's why I felt that if I could hold an opponent to four runs or less the Grays would win.

Sometimes I would see the frustration our opponents experienced when they played us. I'm not saying the Grays were unbeatable, but being a member of Homestead certainly gave one a feeling of comfort. Not financially, but stability-wise in performances.

The Lord has blessed me in so many ways and being a Gray was one of them. I would have never experienced the same success with another team.

Josh Gibson and Buck Leonard, both Grays who eventually became Hall of Famers, played an important part in the career of many ballplayers, mine included. Since Josh was my catcher, and Leonard played first base, we were involved on every pitch. Their philosophy was to win, and they didn't know how to accept losing as just another day at the office. It wasn't just those two either. I remember one time in Philadelphia when I was a 17-year-old rookie, Roy Welmaker, a Grays' pitcher, lost a game 2–1. He got on the bus and he was so angry. Why? One pitch. He wished he could have just one pitch back—the pitch that beat him. Like I said, losing was not a word in the Grays' vocabulary. But the players loved playing for the Grays. In my 11 years with them, I can recall only one player leaving the team because he was dissatisfied, and this was a ballplayer who was homesick for his mother's cooking down in Florida.

Very few ballplayers on the team would show their appreciation verbally. But one player who did, and who was one of the greatest black ballplayers I was ever associated with, was Sam Bankhead—a "true Sam." When he spoke, people listened. He would lift you up when you were down. He went from playing for the Grays to playing and managing. He had a way of telling you about your mistakes without raising his voice or showing any emotion, but, believe me, you got the message loud and clear. One time, he asked me to pitch three times in 24 hours, and I had so much respect for him that I said yes all three times. If ever there was a black ballplayer who should be honored it is Sam Bankhead. Boy, did he know how to make you feel good. I remember a sports writer asked him about the Negro World Series one year between the Birmingham Black Barons and the Grays, and Bankhead said: "If 'Chinky' (my nickname) comes down here we'll win this World Series." To have someone like Bankhead have that much confidence in me gave me a wonderful feeling of stability with the Grays. I think I was relieved only two times between 1939 and 1950 with Homestead.

I got the nickname "Chinky" from the term chinkpin. For city-dwellers, that's a nut that has a fuzzy covering and is brown and yellow. Anyway, I got my nickname in Pennsylvania one hot day. We were playing in Pittsburgh and I was standing on the field with my black and gray jacket on. Buck Leonard was in the dugout and he hollered: "Fields, you look just like a 'Chinkypin.'" That nickname has been with me ever since. We even named our first son "Chinky." So it seems as if Buck Leonard started something on that hot day in Pennsylvania many years ago.

One time, we were traveling through the state of Mississippi at about 4 a.m. and we had to stop and get some gas. Gibson and I were riding up front, and he asked me to go into the diner and get some sandwiches since I am light-skinned. I hesitated for a few seconds and decided the only difficulty I might encounter would be that I would be told to leave the diner. So I went inside and ordered the sandwiches, but another ballplayer, R. T. Walker, stuck his head inside and told me to get him a couple sandwiches too. The proprietor quickly asked me if Walker was with me, and when I said yes, he told me to "get out." After we had departed the premises, Josh told R.T. that he should make him walk to Alabama for ruining his chance for getting some much-deserved food for some starving ballplayers. If we were low on food we would share. Everybody who had food would share with those who didn't, and we'd have what we called a "dutch lunch." It was just like a big family on the Grays.

Sometimes, the Homestead Grays would be traveling in the South and everyone would be hungry and tired so we'd stop at a restaurant. There would be only one black restaurant in certain cities, and this would usually be a small one.

The place would have maybe one cook and one waitress to wait on 17 hungry ballplayers. Now this place was used to serving perhaps a couple customers at any given time, so having an entire hungry ballteam to feed could present problems.

The first few ballplayers to enter the restaurant would be served first, and since the establishment wasn't prepared to serve so many at once it usually meant a shortage of food, or food that was unfavorable. So the ballplayers that didn't eat would walk to the grocery store, which wasn't segregated, and purchase cold cuts and cheese, crackers and pig's feet, tomatoes, and bread, and, of course, something to drink. Hopefully, that food would last a ballplayer all day. At least he'd save a little money by getting food from the grocery store. After everyone returned to the bus, we'd resume our journey. We'd sing songs and play cards to pass the time.

Because the Grays were so well known in the East, South, and Midwest, outsiders would often assist us, which was a gratifying experience. For instance, if the bus broke down, people often would help us get it running again and on the road.

There was never any eating allowed in the dugout. If any food was eaten, it was done in between a double header and in the clubhouse.

There were good and bad hot dogs. I remember when we arrived at a stadium late for a game, we were hungry so we grabbed a couple of quick hot dogs from the concession stand. But the hot dogs turned out to be no good and they had the ballplayers vomiting and trying to play with cramps. And with only 17 players and the stands full of spectators, we played through the sickness in order to assure the money.

Sometimes food was brought on the bus from players' homes. One ballplayer in particular, Bob Thrice, would bring me fried rabbit and chicken. He was a good friend and a gentleman.

Home-cooked food on the bus was a rarity. We used to keep pickled pig's feet under our bus seats. Sometimes we would go without food because there wasn't anywhere to get decent food. But once we'd find a place that had respectable food, we'd patronize that place consistently. Word-of-mouth pointed us to most of the places we ate. Most of the time, the food we'd keep under our bus seats was fresher then a lot of the restaurants we'd try.

Our infield was made up of Leonard, "Lick" Carlisle, "Jelly" Jackson, Chester Williams, Howard Easterling, and Boojum Wilson. That infield was considered one of the best in the Negro Leagues. Our outfield was good, too, and consisted of: Bankhead, Jerry Benjamin, Luke Easter, Luis Marquez, Dave Whatley, and Bob Thurman. Joining Gibson behind the plate was "Eudie" Napier, and my good friend, "Rabroy" Gaston.

Whenever a ballplayer got hurt, a pitcher would replace him. Back in those days, pitchers could do more than just throw the ball. Some of our pitchers could hit the ball with authority. Playing hurt was a way of life in black baseball, and seldom did a new ballplayer join the club. For example, I remember once in 1948, I had just returned from playing ball in San Juan, Puerto Rico, and my arm was so sore I could barely raise it above my head. It was the first time I had ever experienced anything like that. The Grays were playing the Baltimore Elite Giants when I got back, and their club had a rubdown man who agreed to rub my arm for $2.00. That was one time when I got a whole lot for just $2.00, because I pitched against the New York Cubans afterwards and won. When I arrived home in Manassas, I woke my mother and told her the good news, and she said: "God bless you, son."

I went to the doctor only once in 11 years with the Grays. And during my visit, the doctor stuck a long needle into my arm that hit a bone in my elbow. That was the last doctor appointment I ever went to for a baseball injury. The only day the Grays let me have a day off was when the team was getting ready to go to Buffalo for a night game. Vic Harris, our manager at the time, left me in Homestead to get ready to pitch against the Newark Eagles the next night. But I got bombed in that game when I hung a curveball to Monte Pearson in the first inning, and he turned it into a three-run homer. I told Harris never to leave me at home again.

When we expected a large crowd for a game, we'd make sure our uniforms were clean and our shoes were shined. Some ballplayers would use two and three pairs of socks so that their legs would look larger. There was nothing more satisfying than to be in good condition and feel like you were going to win every time you took the field. What's more, pitching for the Homestead Grays was different than pitching for any other team. Since the Grays were noted for their power-hitting ability, which produced a lot of runs, I would always have a positive attitude as I took the mound. I knew that if I could hold a team to four runs or less, I had a better-than-average chance of winning. That knowledge gave me a feeling of security.

However, it wasn't always that way. My first year with Homestead, I was pitching a game in Beaver Falls, Pennsylvania, and every time we'd score a run, the other team would score one also. So, about the sixth inning, Buck Leonard came into the dugout and said: "We have to get someone on the mound who can stop them from hitting." Before he said that, I thought I had been doing a pretty good job. I thought I was doing all right for a 17-year-old country boy, but Buck drilled it into everyone's mind that winning was the only answer on the Grays. That day taught me a valuable lesson: That I would have to crawl before I walked. And it let me know that it wasn't going to be easy to break into the Gray's pitching rotation. The thing is, I didn't mind learning lessons like that, in fact, my experience with the Grays prepared me for 25 years in professional baseball.

Since the players and management always had patience with me, and since it enabled me to do the thing I loved, I was more than glad to accept criticism. If playing in countries around the world and living my life-goal meant taking a lesson now and then, well, that's all right! When a Hall of Famer like Gibson or Leonard had something to say, I listened and learned. Then there was Bankhead: He'd criticize you in such a way that if you listened to him, your future baseball career was going to improve. That's how respected he was. The wisdom that those three shared with me breathed life into my career. I wouldn't change anything in my baseball career, especially the experience and strength I received from that threesome.

Buck Leonard would always remind me what I needed to do to have a successful inning. He would tell me, "You got to stop them from hitting." When he'd stop talking I knew I was doing a good job. He is a true Hall of Famer.

Josh Gibson's criticism was always consistent. He never stopped demanding 100 percent from me. That inspired me to believe that everything is possible if you believe in yourself. He gave me confidence. He is also a true Hall of Famer.

Sam Bankhead gave so much to black baseball and received so little in return. He contributed a great deal to the Grays. When he left there was no replacing him. He was special.

Contract dealings with the Grays were not very pleasant. My contracts were never discussed with the Grays, and certainly never negotiated. They would send me a contract, saying in effect: "Take it or leave it." At the time I broke in with Homestead, my knowledge of the going salaries in the Negro Leagues was limited. And I didn't learn much with time either because players didn't discuss salaries with other players on the team—it might have caused dissension. So the ballplayers were kept in the dark and this benefited the management. The owner and secretary of the Grays did a good job of keeping me unaware of the salaries that were given to other players, and despite my success with them, I was never rewarded. There were other players on the team whose production was below average, but whose salaries exceeded mine. I found this out at the end of my career with the Grays. In Latin American countries, teams would reward you for producing, but not the Grays. In 1946 I went 16–1 for Homestead, and my salary increased by only $100 a month the next season. Luckily, I enjoyed playing the game and being a Gray so much that salaries weren't that big an issue to me.

During those days, other countries were willing and able to pay black players respectable salaries. If only the owners of black baseball clubs had talked to the players signing major league contracts, maybe both sides would have profited more. If the Grays owner or secretary had talked to me about my contract, maybe I would have played baseball elsewhere during my career. As it turned out, I never did become wise with regard to salaries while playing for the Grays. Now I know that salaries increased during my career with the Grays, but back then, nobody let me in on that information. The only time I was ever involved in salary negotiations was when I played ball in Latin American countries and Canada. The reason: I had gathered information about the salaries being paid to former professional players in those countries. Fortunately for me, my play in those countries paid me well enough that the Gray's salary didn't stop me from playing for them. But I can see why other ballplayers would press the owners for more money: they didn't have employment during the winter months in Latin American countries. Not everyone could make it down there, and you better believe if you didn't produce you didn't last long. I was lucky that way.

Some ballplayers went from the Negro Leagues to the majors for financial reasons. They realized that their salaries would remain about the same, but that things couldn't get any worse there. When a black ballplayer played only one position, his salary would be limited. There was always some way a black ballplayer in the Negro Leagues could negotiate for more money with Latin American club owners. It was hard to replace these ballplayers because they were so versatile. Very few ballplayers in the 1940s and 1950s depended solely on one salary in the States.

The Grays maintained financial strength by being a powerhouse ballclub in the Negro Leagues. Homestead gained a reputation for being financially secure, and if they wanted a particular ballplayer, they would find a way to get him. The organization was always prepared for any situation. I can't remember any phase of the organization weakening during my 11 years with it (until the end of the era of the Negro Leagues).

But even at the end, the only visible sign of financial letdown came in 1948 when we were playing the Birmingham Black Barons for the World Series and we agreed to play it down South in Double-A ballclub stadiums instead of our usual major league parks. We only drew four or five thousand spectators in these ballparks, and that was a disaster. If we had played in major league parks we would have had the chance to draw more fans.

When the Grays contacted me in the spring of 1949 and said they planned to hold spring training in Danville, Va., only 240 miles from my home, I sensed that some changes were taking place in the organization. The greatest black team in the U.S. was gone, in its place was a team of uncertain future. So when I reported to the team in Danville, I found out by talking to teammates the reason we had moved to Danville: financial problems.

The team's financial insecurity didn't bother me too much because I had been fortunate enough to have played 12 years of winter ball where I earned a major league salary. But some of my teammates were less fortunate than I was. Not all of them were able to secure a winter job, so I could sense less enthusiasm in camp than in the past.

Finally, my roommate told me that the Grays now belonged to the Southern League, a league that included teams from Richmond, Va., Winston Salem, N.C., and Atlanta, Ga. We could play these teams 10 games, and win all 10. That's when I realized there would be no more Negro National League for Homestead.

In 1949, attendance at the ballpark dropped dramatically for the Grays. Every ballplayer with potential had been picked up by a major league club. The owners had to find other ballplayers with less talent to fill the vacancies. Many positions were left open because the team was unable to fill them respectably. The owners didn't mind this move in one respect because the overall team salary dropped tremendously. But the brand of baseball presented to the fans was less entertaining also. An owner would sell any player to make a dollar.

In 1950, the final season for the Grays, the Grays had a dismal season. I had played ball in Mayagüez, Puerto Rico and had good seasons for them in 1949 and 1950. They offered me a major league salary to play ball for them in the summer, and I thought about the problems the Grays were having, but I decided to play for the Grays again. I reported one month late to the Grays, and when I saw the difficulties the organization was having, I decided to bid farewell to a fine ballclub and organization. I returned to Maracaibo, Venezuela, the team that had hired me for that summer, but first I shook hands with the players and friends of the Grays and wished them well. This wasn't easy to do. After all, it was Buck Leonard and Sam Bankhead who contributed so much to making me a respectable ballplayer. Without the members of the Grays, my life as a professional ballplayer would have been shortlived. I owe everything to them.

The final months of the Homestead Grays were the saddest days of my baseball career. I reminisced about the 1930s and 1940s Grays' teams and the 1950 Grays were a far cry from the fine teams during the peak of the Negro Leagues. But when I departed from the Grays in 1950, I left in good faith. Not only had I contributed to the Negro League, but I am certain that I helped keep the name of the Homestead Grays alive. And for a young country boy who had fantasized about one day playing in the Negro Major Leagues, that meant living a dream come true.

5

Time Out for War

My hitch in the U.S. Army lasted from November 1943 until May 1946, and I'll never regret that experience. It gave me the opportunity to communicate with all difference types of people and deal with all different types of problems. I met soldiers from all over the United States, but it seemed as if most of them came from the Midwest. I took basic training and technical training at Camp Plachea, Louisiana. Those were days of adjustment to rules, regulations, and leadership. I made sergeant in less than 90 days thanks to a bunch of great guys. We made a home away from home together, which helped us overcome what can often be a very hard situation otherwise.

After a while, we boarded a ship in New York and sailed for England. This experience drew us even closer. We left New York harbor on Mother's Day 1944, and I still remember looking out a small ship window as we plunged into the ocean. The Statue of Liberty was the last scene I remember as we sailed away from the shore. Most of us in the company were not prepared for the problems that go with riding a ship across an ocean. I was put in charge of the kitchen duties, and that meant getting used to the ship. One good, sharp turn and we'd find all our kitchen utensils—and sometimes soldiers, too—thrown into one corner of the room, depending on which way the ship had leaned.

We docked in Liverpool, England upon arrival, but we couldn't see anything because of the fog. Eventually, we were able to make out the English docks and nearby surroundings. After departing the ship, we marched through the war-battered streets of Liverpool. The German bombs had done quite some damage. We then boarded freight trains and traveled to a place called Barry Docks, which were located not far from Cardiff, Wales. We were housed for six months in Cardiff, and the barracks there became our home. During that time, our duties included pulling guard duty and unloading arriving ships. Our recreation was limited, but sometimes we played baseball and football on the side of a hill nearby. Also, we had a Red Cross facility where we'd play ping pong and a few other games. I won the ping pong championship of South Wales, England. One time in South Wales, some rubbing alcohol was found while unloading a ship. I can't say everything that happened, but some of the soldiers fought all night and when reveille sounded early the next morning, they stood in formation in just their underwear. I spent the whole day trying to explain to the captain what had happened without anyone getting punished.

I remember one day, a sergeant in our company complained that he had a terrible headache. When he told me how his pain originated, I challenged him right then and there about his ability to drink liquor. I had never had a drink of whiskey until that day. The sergeant said he would buy me 17 drinks of a French whiskey called pastige. This was one of the biggest mistakes I have ever made. I drank the drinks and then I walked back to the barracks. I almost died. This was the first and last time I ever indulged in a whiskey drink.

Our next stop was Marseilles, France. On the trip there, I got sick and lost 30 pounds. I was taken to a hospital in Paris, but that didn't give me much relief, so I was taken back to Marseilles. Soon afterwards, we went across the English Channel and landed on the shores of Le Havre, France, on some sort of mission. Anyway, it looked like plenty of action had taken place there. Once we landed we boarded some vehicles that took us to an open field next to a turnip patch. Since we had been eating spam and jam every day, those turnips sure tasted good to this country boy! One day, we decided to leave our area and do some sightseeing. We had been sleeping in mud and we felt the need to move. Anyway, we walked for a while and then spotted a small church that was quite a building to behold, so we went on in and prayed. Next thing you know, we had fallen asleep; that's how tired we were. After we got back to camp, we boarded some boxcars and headed back to Marseilles. We were placed in an old, bombed-out building that had no windows and had blankets for beds. The temperature was below-freezing, so I didn't take off my socks for 11 days. When I finally did, my feet were so tender that nothing could touch them.

While in France, we had Frenchmen helping us to unload ships. They would bring a bottle of wine and a piece of French bread for lunch. Food was very scarce and they would offer the American soldiers whatever they had to eat. They didn't know that we were without food for long periods of time. Neither one of us complained about the conditions that existed for a worthy reason: We were trying to win a war. I can't remember one fight between the French and Americans.

While we were stationed at Marseilles, the company chose a couple of us to take some rest and relaxation in Nice, France. They chose us on the basis of what we had contributed to the company. I really appreciated that vacation.

After returning to camp, we received orders to prepare for duty in the Pacific. The war was over in Europe and we were sent to a staging area to get ready to depart for the Pacific. The soldiers said they would follow me anywhere. I felt real good about that. Knowing that I had contributed to the soldiers' well-being and that they would possibly keep those memories forever was special. Over 40 years later, I can still see some of the faces of my buddies and I reminisce about our good and bad times.

While at the staging area, I came in contact with a hospital outfit that was made up completely of white soldiers. I was put in touch with the first sergeant who asked me if I knew of any company that played baseball in the area. It turned out this company had a baseball team that had been together for several years. I told him that maybe we could play his company, so we scheduled a game. We played on a former battleground in France, and we beat them 5–0. The first sergeant asked me to join his company and go to Japan with them. Apparently, he knew the right people to make this come about. But before anything happened an order came down for my company to sail for the States: The Japanese had surrendered!

Sailing home from France was another experience that will stay with me forever. We were four or five days in the Atlantic when a storm hit us. It was so severe that the ship couldn't move, so we had to change course and take a different route home. Instead of landing in New York, we had to land in Boston. When we disembarked there my mind went over the many trials and tribulations that we had confronted and come through. It was good to be back in America!

During my Army career, I found out that the lessons my parents taught me would play an important part in dealing with unpleasant situations that existed from time to time. One lesson in particular that my parents taught me was that it was imperative to appreciate other people. The ability to converse with a high official or a private in the military was my ultimate goal. This is why a captain tried to get me to reinlist so that I would become a first sergeant of a company. The

Army taught me never to ask someone to do something that you wouldn't do yourself. Treat every person as a human being, and don't lie to make yourself superior or important.

Upon my arrival in America, I received a telegram saying my father had had a major operation. In two days I had secured a 30-day furlough. Since it was harvest time, it was a good time for me to go home. My dad survived the ulcer operation, and I harvested his corn and hay crop. He was so pleased, and I felt so good inside to be able to help him—a truly deserving man. It allowed me to repay a small portion of the good life he had given me.

After my furlough was up, the Army sent me to Camp Plachea again. It wasn't far from New Orleans, and my stay there was a memorable one. This is where I first met my wife, Audrey. I went to see her every night. She came from a large family where love and discipline were a way of life. Audrey and I were married before I left New Orleans to be discharged at Fort Meade, Maryland. I talked with Audrey every day and night.

6

Saying No to the Majors

In 1946, a scout approached me after I had pitched a shutout against the New York Black Yankees in Yankee Stadium. He asked me if I would like to play ball for Montreal, the Triple-A club of the Brooklyn Dodgers. I told him no, that I wasn't interested.

In 1948 the Yankees offered me a contract to play in their organization in Oakland, California. Charlie Dressen was the manager there, and he called me very night for a week. The Yankees even offered me a bonus on top of the contract just to sign. Finally, I agreed. I told Dressen that I would join the club in one week. He sent me plane fare and travel expenses. I asked my sister Evelyn to take me to the airport. We got as far as Seven Corners in Arlington, Virginia—not far from the airport—when I told her to turn the car around and head home. I sent the money back to Dressen that same day. It took 40 years, but I finally found out that Audrey was glad I didn't go to California.

I got two more major league offers: one from the Washington Senators in 1949, and one from the St. Louis Browns organization in 1952.

That brings up the question that I've always been asked by inquisitive baseball fans: Why? Why did I turn down major league contracts in order to stay in the black leagues? The answer is simple: Ever since I was a 10-year-old, day-dreaming boy who walked down those dusty roads praying I'd someday play black baseball, that was my great hope in life. When the contracts were finally offered to me from the major leagues, I'd already landed in the middle of my dream—black professional baseball—and by then I had a family. I had to ask myself if switching would benefit my family. I decided it would not. It wasn't worth the risk of jeopardizing my family's well-being, because at that point I was playing three or four games weekly for a salary (including winter ball) that exceeded most major league salaries. I was able to make such a salary by going South in the winter, like many of my Negro League counterparts.

The most successful ballplayers in the 1930s through 1950s were the black ones who maintained winter baseball jobs in Latin American countries. It was ridiculous for a ballplayer to think that he could survive the winter months in the States without a job. A Negro League ballplayer couldn't save anything from his summer employment. So when springtime rolled around, many a black ballplayer was relieved because he knew his finances would again be taken care of. Therefore, it was inevitable and logical that we had to play ball in the winter and the summer in order to make ends meet. But the biggest thrill of all was knowing that I had a successful winter playing ball, which meant my services would be in demand again the next winter.

Monte Irvin, now a Hall of Famer and a former Major League executive, played baseball in San Juan, Puerto Rico, in 1946. When the owners of the club he played for came to the U.S. looking for some more imports for their team, Monte recommended me to them. After that I just kept going, going, going, and I went just about everywhere to play baseball.

If a ballplayer could handle more than one position, he had the capability to negotiate a higher salary. I'm glad I played as many positions as I could with the Grays because that experience allowed me to be one of the fortunate ones who were able to play in Latin America, where versatility was valued. All told, I played 12 seasons there. I played three or four games a week and made more money a month than I was offered for a month by the major leagues. So, it's apparent why I wasn't hurrying to jump into the majors. I was offered $2,200 a month to play in the Dominican Republic in 1952, yet I was offered $4,000 for the entire season to sign a big-league contract that same year.

When my wife and I arrived in San Juan, Puerto Rico, in 1947, it was a totally different experience from anything I'd ever been involved in. The people there accepted us as leaders and people who could bring them a baseball championship. If an import like myself didn't produce immediately, on the other hand, his stay would be short-lived. I always asked myself, "Am I doing enough to stay here?" The fans always generated enough negative feelings to let it be known if they weren't satisfied with a player's performance. When I first got to San Juan, the team was in last place, which makes it harder to please the fans. That meant I had to try even harder to play well. I was fortunate enough to put together two outstanding weeks. My confidence grew stronger and I saw the fans recognize the talent that I possessed. That made my first year there a successful one—I hit .328 and went 5–5 on the mound for a last-place ballclub—and it created a foundation to play in Latin American countries. When a player was named to an all-star team or picked to play in the Caribbean Series, that gave him the ability to negotiate for a better contract.

When I returned home from that first season, I had time to evaluate my stay there and I thought back on the positive things that were said about me. I was named "Player of the Week" two weeks in a row for San Juan, and the papers named me "Wilmer Fields the Great." That season established a relationship between me and the owner of the Puerto Rican club that enabled me to play 12 seasons in Puerto Rico, Venezuela, Colombia, Dominican Republic, Cuba, and Panama. The owners trusted me to such a degree that they'd send me as much as $5,000 before leaving the United States.

Traveling to Puerto Rico that first year was the first time Audrey and I rode an airplane. The trip was hard, too. We left New York City at 3 p.m. and didn't get to San Juan until 6 a.m. the next morning. Traveling by plane down there in the 1940s and 1950s wasn't something you wanted to remember. We traveled in two-engine planes over the Andes Mountains that were quite unstable. I know one ballplayer who would drink alcohol on a trip. Of course, he didn't know if he was on the ground or up in the air. Most clubs tried to keep the cost of transportation as low as possible. But after establishing himself, a player could demand better travel arrangements.

Playing ball in Puerto Rico certainly meant making some adjustments. But playing there also brought many fine associations with people as well. My wife and I stayed on a narrow street in the middle of San Juan. Segregation was not an issue down there. We went to movies and restaurants freely, and when I was on the baseball field, no unpleasant words were directed at me. Still, I was glad to return home after four months so I could eat some home cooking.

In 1948 I played ball for Mayagüez, Puerto Rico, and, again, there weren't any signs of discrimination. We played four games a week there: one on Saturday, two on Sunday, and one on Tuesday. It could get as hot as a fire in Puerto Rico, especially if you were pitching. I lost as many as 12 pounds one game while going nine innings. I got cramps from the bottom of my feet to the tip of my tongue. The team showered before me and used all the hot water, so I decided to take a cold shower which turned out to be a near-fatal mistake.

In Mayagüez, we stayed in a house five minutes from the ballpark. Travel down there was done by rental cars, and the longest road trip was three hours. In Puerto Rico I pitched, played the outfield, third base, and shortstop. The owner of the Mayagüez Indians ballclub was a man named Valdez. He was a millionaire who owned the electric company and an Indian beer company. He would invite the ballplayers to his mansion on a hill every Christmas, and he'd give every player the gift of one week's salary. He even came to Washington, D.C. in 1948 to talk to me about playing for him that year.

The baseball owners in Latin American countries trusted me so much that they would have me secure players for their teams. I would negotiate salaries and then document a contract for a given salary before a player would leave the States. I was lucky that no player ever crossed me in fulfilling his contract. If you ever crossed an owner, they became very reluctant to deal with you again. I remember one ballplayer who played in Mexico. He'd been down there a month when he asked the owner if he could go home to attend his mother's funeral in Chicago. The owner not only gave him permission, but he even advanced the player some money. The player returned after the funeral, and about two months later approached the owner under the same circumstances. The owner said: "How many funerals is your mother going to have?" Needless to say, that player had violated the owner's trust, and he had a hard time after that.

If you relate the amount of money that players were getting advanced in those days to today's standards, ballplayers were getting the equivalent of $20,000 or more in advance. But I think the owners knew they could be reimbursed if a player didn't fulfill a contract obligation by spreading the word around to other owners. Word traveled fast in Latin American countries, so if a player wanted to ruin his future down there, all he had to do was let one owner down. The system was good to me because it maintained my career the same way it hurt others. The word-of-mouth communication between owners gave me the privilege of playing baseball in Latin American countries!

It was very hard to maintain good eating habits in Latin America. To get the food necessary to keep me fit was almost impossible. I'd lose so much weight that my clothes would look like bags on me. The temperature would be about 100 degrees and there was no shade.

When I thought about playing under those conditions it made me miserable, so I tried not to think about it too much. Once I lost the weight it was difficult to regain it. But whenever I thought about my overall situation, I realized I had to take the bitter with the sweet. When I'd return to the States and home, my weight would balloon back within two weeks. I'd stay at home anywhere from one to three months and then start the process all over again.

The first week of adjusting to the weather conditions in Latin America was the hardest for me. Sometimes, I'd be on my hands and knees while trying to survive on the baseball fields. Later on, my physical and mental stability would strengthen. Regardless of what you had done in the past, the fans expected a super year from you immediately. So you always had a good feeling after a successful season because you knew your performance had ensured you a future job with that club. And as long as I was having a good season in a country, the accommodations for my family were prioritized. I often wonder if today's black ballplayers could survive some of the conditions and circumstances that existed in the 1930s and 1940s.

I was fortunate enough to appear on radio and television in Latin America. In San Juan, when I was named "Player of the Week," the theater in town would honor my wife and me with gifts and money. In the Dominican Republic, we were honored by a television station that interviewed me on the prospects of Latin American baseball. And in Canada, the interviews usually focused on my past credentials as they knew I had played with the Homestead Grays in the summers, and Latin American countries in the winters. The stations gave me copies of those interviews.

I was lucky enough to play in several Caribbean Series, which are Latin America's version of post-season play. The Series consisted of teams from Venezuela, Cuba, Panama, and Puerto Rico. In 1949 our team from Mayagüez represented Puerto Rico while the Series was played in Cuba. Cuba was the favorite and was picked to win the Series based on the Cuban and American ballplayers who made up their roster. And they did win easily.

In 1950 I was selected by Caguas of Puerto Rico to play for them in the Caribbean Series, this time in Puerto Rico. Every team in the Series had the opportunity to select one player from any team in the league. Again, Cuba was the favorite, but this time they didn't win it. I pitched against them and gave up three hits. Again, Cuba was made up mostly of major league players that year. In one game, I pinch hit a home run in the ninth inning to beat Venezuela. Panama eventually won the Series by beating Dan Bankhead of our team.

In Latin America and Canada, your name became the topic of daily discussions by the fans. At first, they discussed your potential as a permanent ballplayer. Once you were established you were set. Once, after that good Caribbean Series in 1950, a club from Maracaibo, Venezuela handed me one month's salary in advance of the next season to play two games a week at $1,500 a week with all expenses paid. It was good to feel wanted and trusted like this.

I remember playing with Mayagüez in the Caribbean Series in 1949, and I'll never forget that Chuck Conners—of the TV show "Rifleman"—was playing first base for Cuba. He chose the right profession when he decided on acting. Playing against Cuban teams was like playing against teams in the States. Everyone spoke English and conversations were easily understood. And Cuban fans seemed to be more aware of what was going on in the world of baseball than did many of the other country's fans. The Latin American countries considered Cuba the premier country for baseball. This was because major league clubs like the Washington Senators and others would get several of their players from Cuba. Cuba's baseball reputation was well-known throughout the world.

The third and final Caribbean Series I played in was 1952 for Caracas, Venezuela. Our team had finished the regular season 12 games in first place, and was made up mostly of Triple-A U.S. players and four Venezuelans. I had a good year and had been voted the Most Valuable Player while leading the league in batting, home runs, runs batted-in, and runs scored. But, again, we came up short in the Series. It was during this Series that I was contacted by several major league scouts who were interested in my services, but I had already signed with Jack Kent Cooke, the current owner of the Washington Redskins, who owned a Canadian baseball team at the time.

I played ball on four teams that were predominantly white. In Caracas, Venezuela, we had eight imports on the team, and seven of them were white. All of us and our families stayed in the same hotel and we took our meals together. We would play cards together and sometimes the games would last all day. We respected each other.

On other teams, we had our separate homes. The only time we saw each other was when we played a game. I have no regrets about being a member of a mostly white baseball team.

The revolution in Puerto Rico in 1950 changed my mind about

how long I'd play baseball in that country. Although we weren't hurt, it was an experience I'll never forget. Being from a small town in Virginia, I wasn't accustomed to this type of thing. When the shooting stopped and we thought we had a chance to reach San Juan, my wife and daughter drove there. We put our car on a boat and took the first plane to Miami. The revolution was during the season, and that ended four prosperous seasons in Puerto Rico. It was time to move on anyway because after a player had been in one place for a while, salary increases were harder to come by.

7

North of the Border

I first played in Canada in the summer of 1952. I played there five years all together. I hit .300, .381, .382, .379, and .425, and was MVP three times. There was no comparison between the treatment we received in Canada and the treatment we received in Latin America. In Canada, it was like a home away from home. The Canadians would invite us to their homes. My family could go to the movies free. Steak dinners were given to me every time I hit a home run. We would go golfing and fishing together. One family would phone us everyday. The owners of the club offered me an opportunity to own a sporting goods store.

In Latin American countries, everything was business. If I produced, my financial status would improve. Money was the name of the game in Latin American countries. This was the main reason I pitched and played the outfield and infield. When I played more than one position my salary would double. Latin American countries would give me extra money if I played outstandingly. They would also give me money in advance on my salary before I left the States.

The Canadian people also wanted ballplayers who represented their city and their community off the field as well as on the field. It was a good feeling. The people there accepted my family with so much enthusiasm that our stay there was the finest we ever experienced anywhere but at our home. A lot of thanks goes to club owners Mike King, Larry Pennell, and Art Holman; they made life especially comfortable for us.

I remember one day in Canada when Clifford and Richardson and I were going to the ballpark. We were driving through the neighborhood and we passed a couple of young white boys who were playing in their front yard. As we went by, one of the boys hollered out "Nigger." I stopped the car and went up and knocked on the front door of their house. I was hoping to speak with their father, but a woman answered the door. I asked her if the children were hers, and she said they were. I told her what happened and she apologized and had the boys do the same. At least this was a step toward improving the relationship between Canadian families and the few black families that were living in the well-respected neighborhood. It took only a couple of minutes of time but it was well worth it. We continued on our journey without remorse. What the boys said surprised us. After all, this was my family's second home—where my family almost made our permanent residence.

My first Canadian club was Brantford, Ontario. This was also my first experience with the game of golf. The fishing was terrific, too. The people there invited us into their homes and this made for a relaxing atmosphere. I remember our oldest son, "Chinky," decided he was going to get some bread from our neighbors. She gave him the bread and Chinky had himself a snack. We became good friends with the neighbor and I still laugh when I think about that episode.

The people in Brantford were so good to us that they even wanted to set us up in a sporting goods store. The best part of the deal was I didn't have to put any money up to start. There's no doubt in my mind that if I had chosen to go along with this adventure it would have been a success. But we had built our house in Manassas and that's where our roots were. I regret that I didn't accept that business offer because the person who finally did open the sporting goods business ended up making $500,000 a year with it.

I returned to Canada after I had ended my career for an Old-Timer's Game. The people gave me an unbelievable welcome. I hit a home run during the game and it was a thrill because it allowed me to give back something to the dedicated fans. Some of our friends are still living in the same neighborhoods as they were in the 1950s. While we were there, I saw a newspaper article on the sports page that reviewed the contributions of several Brantford players since 1946. Some of the players even went on to play in the major leagues. In the article, a part-owner of Brantford, Mr. Larry Pennell, who was also a judge and Attorney General of Ontario, gave the journalist his opinion on the past ballplayers. He said: "There were several outstanding players in the league, but the greatest of all was Wilmer Fields." I brought that newspaper home and my wife and daughter framed it for me.

So many generous people came into our lives in Canada. One year there, I got to know the manager of the drive-in theater. He would wave us in without accepting pay. My children looked forward to these outings because they were fun and Audrey would fix snacks to take along. Another "extra" in Canada was a restaurant that would give a steak dinner for every home run. We ate a few of those, too.

After my first season in Canada, I went to Caracas, Venezuela, for the winter. I made more money in Caracas than Puerto Rico, and the living conditions and food were better too. I was more satisfied in Caracas than any Latin American country that I had played in. But, like Puerto Rico, Venezuela had just witnessed a revolution, and this one saw the country's President killed. That was scary.

In Caracas, we played three games a week. I played third base next to Chico Carrasquel, who played shortstop for the Chicago White Sox for many years. His father used to pitch for the Washington Senators. The weather was nice in Caracas during the day, and at night stayed around 70 degrees. This was the winter, mind you. The weather must have agreed with me because I was named MVP that year.

When I played in Maracaibo, Venezuela, we played the same number of games per week, but the weather was unbearable at times. We didn't have any air conditioning, but somehow my wife and daughter managed to survive there in 1950. I pitched and played the outfield, and the outfield had a lot of sand in it. The sand would get so hot that my feet would get burned right through my shoes. After each inning I'd take my shoes off and dip my feet in water to cool them off. Luis Aparicio, who went on to the White Sox and was an all-star shortstop for several years, used to buy us snowballs to eat. I treated him like my son. His father played on our team. The food in Maracaibo wasn't the greatest unless you loved rice and beans. It wasn't my fantasy. Audrey and my daughter Maridel used to walk to get banana splits and, boy, were those a treat. Probably, if I had known about the Venezuelan revolution, I would have had a different opinion about going there to play regardless of the money involved. We were lucky to arrive after it had ended.

I hit .397 that season and as a result, the owner asked me back. Since we played only three games a week, I had plenty of time to improve my golf game and catch a few big ones out of the creeks.

I remember one year in Venezuela when our club was made up of exports and players with Double- and Triple-A experience. The rest of the club was made up of established imports and Venezuelans.

Anyway, the newspaper picked us to finish last, but we ended up winning our first 17 games, and finishing with a 10-game lead. That was one of the most enjoyable seasons that I was ever a part of.

The Wordolf Hotel was our home in Venezuela. All of the imported ballplayers stayed there with their families. We had eight white Americans from major league organizations on our team and we were just like a big family. I earned the MVP award in that season.

Next, it was back to Canada again, only this time under less wonderful circumstances. This is when I played for Jack Kent Cooke. I was told that Mr. Cooke wanted to meet with me. I wondered why he wanted to see me, and different thoughts ran through my mind. It turned out that he wanted me to play Triple-A baseball for his team in Toronto. We met for about 45 minutes, but we reached no agreement. In fact, when I left his office I forgot all about our conversation. I finished the 1951 season at Brantford, went home for a month of rest, then took off for Caracas for the winter league. I arrived in Caracas about a week before the season began on Oct. 15, and I was relaxed and looking forward to another good season.

One of the players on the team that year was one of Mr. Cooke's players from the previous season. Apparently, Mr. Cooke had informed the player of our conversation in Canada, because this player asked me if I was interested in playing in Toronto the next summer. I told him I'd let him know. Anyway, during the next two weeks, Mr. Cooke called me every other day from Toronto. I spoke with Audrey about possibly signing a contract with Mr. Cooke. He was offering a $5,000 signing bonus on top of a major league contract, and he agreed to pay for my wife to make all trips while I played for Toronto. I decided to accept Mr. Cooke's offer. We agreed by telephone that he would send me a telegram containing all the details of my contract. After receiving his telegram, I sent him one back—not knowing that by doing so I was in effect signing a contract—saying I accepted his offer.

In between the time I agreed to play for Mr. Cooke and the end of the Venezuelan season, I decided I didn't want to play for him in the summer. I talked to him several times about this, but because of my telegram, he maintained I was obligated to play for him. I hired a Canadian lawyer and a lawyer in Columbus, Ohio, to try and get me out of that contract, but I was told that ignorance of the law was no excuse for accepting a contract by telegram. So I lost the battle and my services belonged to Mr. Cooke.

I went home and Mr. Cooke called me and asked me if I'd come to Toronto to talk with him about the agreement. He paid for all expenses and even sent a limousine to Buffalo, New York, to pick me up from there. When I arrived at Mr. Cooke's office, he was waiting with a smile and a handshake. We spoke for approximately two hours and we talked about everything, even things from his personal life which I never have, and never will, reveal to anyone. It didn't help me get out of the contract, though. When he wanted something, he got it. At one point, I even tried to give him money to cancel the contract, but he didn't want it. Fighting him would have been like fighting Wall Street. After all, he didn't get to be a millionaire at the age of 32 by being dumb.

The Triple-A club in Toronto belonged to the International League, and it was a step below the major leagues. I was 30 years old at that time. Some people predicted I would hit .300 with 25 home runs, and drive in 90 or more RBIs, but I never reached my potential there. I broke my wrist that summer and still hit the ball pretty well when I returned to the team. I hit in the cleanup position and hit .300 until the last day of the season when pitcher Johnny Podres of the Dodgers held me hitless. In 1953 I jumped to the Dominican Republic because after the Latin American countries found out about my wrist injury, they weren't as interested in my services. Mr. Cooke said I was ineligible to play in any organized league of baseball because I had left his team. At this point, I decided to challenge the rules concerning baseball players' rights by going to the Dominican Republic despite Mr. Cooke's declaration.

The Dominican Republic treated my family well in 1953. There were only two black imports on the San Pedro de Macoris club I played for, and the rest were Latin Americans. We were given a house and the rest of the accommodations were well planned for. Some Cuban ballplayers made some unkind remarks that I ignored, and for the most part our stay was a pleasant one. We had four teams in the league, and our longest road trip was four hours. We played three games a week, and my salary was the highest I ever received playing baseball: salary and expenses equaling $3,000 a month.

We would basically play one game on Saturday and then two on Sunday. I was hitting .392 and everything was going well baseball-wise, but my children were on the verge of becoming really sick, so I asked the owners to let me go home. I owed the club $1,300 from the two month's advance they had given me. The owner tried to persuade me to stay but once he saw my mind was made up, he accepted his money and let me go. I enjoyed the Dominican Republic, and I even got to meet the president of the country. He was a friend of the owner.

I played two more summers in Canada, and they were with Brantford in 1954 and 1955. I believe this was one country where I could have started and ended my baseball career. We were always treated with respect even though there were only three black families in Ontario while I played there. I will not attempt to name all the Canadian people we are grateful to, but our memories of them and Canada will live forever.

Here I am as a member of the Homestead Grays in 1946, the year of my best pitching record in black baseball (16–1).

The 1947 Grays were a machine that relied on pitching, hitting, fielding, and speed to make it go. What a thrill it was to be part of this organization.

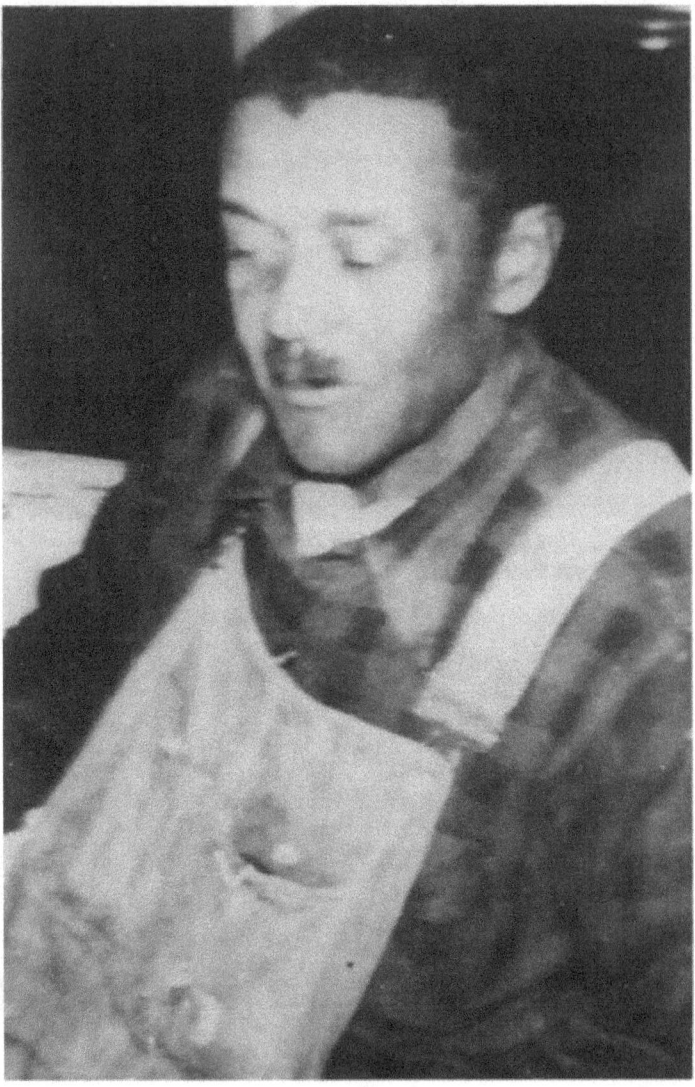

There is only one thing I can say about my father: he is the greatest person I have ever known and everything a father should be. He is in my prayers every day.

A person of love and determination, my mother thought that there was nothing too good for her children. She organized our lives and provided us with a wealth of love. A great mother, my mom deserved the respect of everyone.

Receiving a football scholarship from Virginia State College was an honor. Few scholarships were given to blacks in the 1930s. Despite the football scholarship, my dream was to someday play professional baseball.

Being just 17 years old when I joined the Homestead Grays, it was hard to figure out what the team expected of me. A rookie ballplayer is like a young plant that must be handled properly if it is to reach its maturity and potential. With proper handling, the plant will thrive.

The full roster of the Homestead Grays, with me on the left.

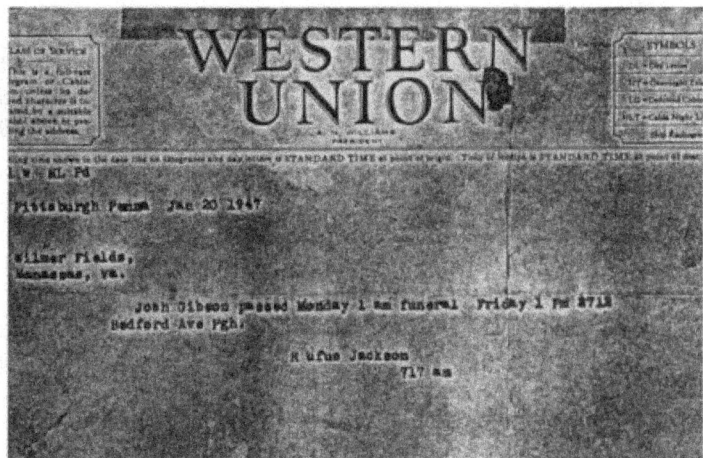

A dear friend of mine, a Hall of Fame member, my riding partner on the bus, and my catcher, Josh Gibson inspired me many times by saying, "You can do it, Chinky!" He was one of the greatest hitters of all time, and his passing has left me with many memories.

THE EAST ALL-STARS OF 1948

The East All-Stars of 1948, with Newark Eagles, New York Cuban Stars.

This picture was enlarged from a baseball card in Mayaguez, Puerto Rico. The card was given to me when I attended a reunion of black ballplayers in Baltimore.

The 1948–1949 Puerto Rican champion club I was a member of was defeated in the Caribbean Series by a Cuban club. The Puerto Rican team had more talent than any Latin American club that I ever played on. It provided me with some fond memories.

I arrived in the Dominican Republic in 1953 with my wife Audrey and our two children. It was an interesting experience because this was our first visit to the country and with the salary they were paying me to play three games a week, I knew it would be difficult adjusting to the conditions there.

Greeting teammate Luke Easter after his hitting a home run at Griffith Stadium in Washington, D.C. Luke later played for the Cleveland Indians. It was a good feeling to share things with Luke, like hitting the ball with authority.

I was honored as the best ballplayer in Ontario by the Attorney General of Ontario, who was once a part-owner of the club there.

In 1955, I played ball for a team in Barranquila, Colombia. We had eight Americans on the team. These imports were from the Cincinnati Reds' organization.

This was taken before playing a game in Fort Wayne, Indiana, in 1956. I hit .427 that year—one of my best efforts.

This picture was taken during one of my eight years working in the Little League. We won the championship six out of eight years. I will never forget those times. Our team was like a large, happy family, and the boys never gave me any trouble.

The Philadelphia Phillies honored some of the "Black Legends of Baseball" during a Pirates-Phillies ballgame in 1990. Some of these players still live in the Philadelphia area.

My wife and I attending our daughter's wedding

Our son Marvin, whose nickname was "Chinky," could have made it in pro baseball. At the age of 16, he had hop on his fastball. I don't think he realized the talent and potential he had.

Our daughter Maridel.

Our youngest son Billy, who played four years on a basketball scholarship at Providence College.

Our granddaughters Michelle and Renee.

 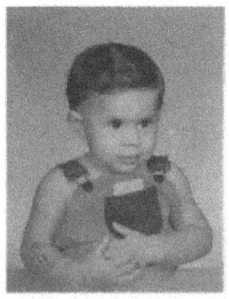 

Our grandsons Brandon, Andrew, and Mark Anthony.

A reunion of the black players in Ashland, Kentucky, in 1984 was the beginning of these players gaining recognition for their achievements. What a feeling to be reunited with faces I hadn't seen for forty years. Each face represented a different story, a different memory.

In 1988, the Pittsburgh Pirates' organization honored the Homestead Grays' 1948 World Champions. That was the last year the Grays were a part of the Negro National League.

8
The End of the Road

My next stop was Colombia, South America, where I played during the winter of 1955–56. I guess they were pleased with me down there, because the owner offered me the managing job. I turned it down because I felt that since I was the only black import on the team, there might have been a letdown from some of the other imports. Back in those days it was hard to make some decisions because situations like these were hard to figure out.

I can't remember a lot of discrimination occurring while we were there, but I do remember some of the white imports not appreciating us eating at the same table as their families.

Before retiring, I played a season at Fort Wayne, Indiana, where I hit .430 and had a 4–1 record in 1956, and then I went back to Colombia that winter. My last two seasons were spent with St. Joe, Michigan, and the Mexico City Reds in 1957 and 1958, respectively. I hit .390 with St. Joe and .398 for the Reds.

St. Joe was a team I really enjoyed playing for. The owner, Mr. Tisonia, was a real gentleman. He was a millionaire and he showed his appreciation when a ballplayer produced. He even offered me a year-round job. He paid me a major-league salary and was one owner to whom I felt indebted. He was a respectable human being in every way.

I consider myself to be lucky to have played baseball in Latin American countries and Canada for so many years. I was fortunate to be part of a system that showed appreciation for your abilities as a ballplayer regardless of your color. I wish the black teams in the United States paid a salary equal to a person's value like teams in other countries did.

Despite the abuse that I encountered from time to time I kept going because I felt my day would come, and it did in every respect. Abuse just gave me that much more incentive to try harder. If I wrote every time that I had asked God to help me along the way, this book would never be able to contain the countless prayers that I have prayed. The Lord has always made a way for me to accomplish goals in my life. Believing and having faith has been the foundation of my life.

9
Lessons Learned

Learning how to do certain important things in baseball took time, but once I discovered that certain abilities made me a better player, which meant more money, I worked hard to improve those aspects of my game. The ability to hit a curveball or run the bases well are a couple of examples. Through effort and determination I learned to hit the breaking ball, and, as a matter of fact, ended up hitting more home runs off curves than I did off the fastball. Another valuable lesson I learned was the ability to play more than one position. Playing several positions not only lessened the pressure to perform well at just one thing, but I am convinced it increased the length of my career by a number of years. And it all began one day with the Grays. Sam Bankhead told Vic Harris to let me play third base, and that was the start of a long career as an infielder.

But, first, I had to learn the position. That's where the studying and extra practice paid off. There was never a time while I was playing baseball that I wasn't trying to improve. Whether it was learning to play a different position, or trying out different hitting techniques, I was always striving to get better. I remember an old-timer telling me: "Chinky always be ready at the plate and never let your chance pass you by." I used to move around in the batter's box in order to adjust to certain types of pitches. Oddly enough, one of my faults that followed me throughout my career was, at the same time, one of the reasons I played as long as I did: I took things for granted. If I didn't succeed on the mound, then I felt like my ability to accomplish other goals, or to play other positions, was always available to me. I often wonder how successful I would have been had I played only one position.

By playing so many positions, perhaps I never realized the full value of what I might have been able to do on the field. But I can say that all my wants were satisfied. I made decisions by looking at what was in the best interest of my family. As I look back at all the opportunities that passed me by to improve myself in baseball, but that I let go because my family always came first, it made me realize that everything in life carries a price tag. And I paid the price.

But regardless of what position I played, I was always known as a tough competitor who was determined and dedicated. "Pee Wee" Butts of the Baltimore Elite Giants knew this when he said: "Chinky never quits." This was the type of attitude a player had to maintain in order to succeed. Respect for others meant a great deal to me in life. No one in life should be overlooked, regardless of whether his or her individual gift is a large one or a small one.

I found out early in my pitching career that it took more than just throwing the ball to a catcher. Control is the main ingredient for any successful pitcher. When I first joined the Homestead Grays at age 17, my manager, Vic Harris, would always remind me of the importance of good control to a pitcher. If a pitcher didn't have a pitch he could throw consistently for a strike, he would say, his days of struggle will last a long time. I would try to see how many fastballs I could throw in a row without throwing a ball. Of course, this was before a ballgame. My control allowed me to throw a 90-mile-per-hour fastball anywhere I wanted for a strike. High, low, inside, or outside, it didn't matter.

After gaining control of my fastball, I added a curveball to my repertoire. Throwing a curveball was somewhat like throwing a fastball, in that unless a pitcher throws it for a strike, he'll have problems with even mediocre hitters. Sometimes I'd throw my curveball more like a slider, and other times like a big curve. As my career progressed, and I gained more confidence with my two pitches, I decided I needed a third option, especially for those times when my other pitches weren't working. So I watched an old-timer for the Grays, Raymond Brown, throw his outstanding knuckleball, and I worked with him for several years while learning to throw one myself. Eventually, I got to the point where I could throw one consistently, and I had my third pitch. A running knuckleball is one of the hardest pitches to hit in baseball. One time I threw a knuckler to a batter in Canada who swung at the pitch, but the darn ball went between his legs and he wasn't even drinking.

Sometimes, I'd feel real good warming up and yet have trouble getting past the fifth inning. Luckily, that didn't happen too often. To this day, I can remember the teams or hitters that gave me a hard time. After a game, I would look back at the mistakes I had made, and my immediate goal would be to correct them.

One night during a ballgame in Canada it snowed after the temperature dropped real fast. Our team had a loaded bat that weighed about 10 ounces more than the bat I usually used. I usually hit the ball to left field, but with that bat the ball would be hit to right.

I hated the cold weather when I was hitting. But when I was pitching it was an entirely different story. My fastball would sting the hitters' hands when I pitched on the inside of the plate and make it difficult for them to hit the ball solidly.

There is no comparison between black baseball players in the 1930s and 1940s and the players of today. The teaching and treatment that players receive today are a hundred times better than back then. When I see today's players making millions of dollars a season, I wonder if some of them could have even played professionally back then. I don't see the players of today trying to improve themselves as much as they could because of the amount of money they're making. If a player hit .200 in the 1930s or 1940s, he wouldn't have lasted, no matter how good a fielder he was. But, nowadays some .200 hitters are making hundreds of thousands of dollars a season. The love of the game, and playing for the sake of the game itself, has been lost. Obviously, if players are going to be awarded sky-high contracts regardless of production, their incentive to be the best they can be is decreased.

Hitters that are unable to adjust to different pitches and their location will never hit for average. The only way this type of hitter can succeed is if a pitcher makes a mistake. The belief that a hitter will "get his pitch every time at the plate if he's patient" is false. If a pitcher is patient and pitches to a hitter's weakness, he will get him out most of the time. A good hitter can adjust his style of hitting to hit all pitchers. Maybe not with authority, but good enough to get on base.

We had poor hitters in the black leagues just as they do in the majors. But we had what were considered poor hitters in the black leagues leave us and go to the majors and become stars. And I know that other black players could have gone to the majors, but were never given the opportunity.

It was always an advantage to me to be able to see a pitcher more than once. I never forgot a pitcher's best pitches. If a pitcher succeeded in getting me out the first time I faced him, you could bet your last dollar I would be waiting for him the next time. This is why hitting is often a guessing game. But if a pitcher has three good pitches that he can throw with command anytime he wants, hitting becomes much more difficult.

Very few hitters go from being poor hitters to good ones. Why? Because they can't adjust their style of hitting. I would have never been satisfied if I hit below .250 like you see players do often these days. In fact, I would not be playing back then if I hit under .250. You just didn't do that and stick around for long.

The most difficult task for me when I played ball was to face a player or a team that I had never seen before. I liked to study my opposition so I could figure out what strategy to use against them based on their strong and weak points. Whenever possible, I tried to remember every pitch I threw to a hitter. There were two hitters who made it difficult for me as a pitcher: Larry Doby, who went on to play for the Cleveland Indians, and "Home Run" Willard Brown. Brown played in the majors, too. Both of them gave me a hard time, and it didn't matter what I threw them.

Over my career, I gathered knowledge about pitching that helped me tremendously. My philosophy was not to allow .220 hitters to reach base. Nowadays, there are so many of those types of hitters. Of course, the consistent .300 hitters were going to get their hits no matter what, so it was absolutely imperative not to allow the lesser hitters to hurt you. If I hung a curveball to a .220 hitter, the pain would last a long time. So my ambition was to make sure I got the hitters I was supposed to.

Back when I played ball, the home teams would supply two dozen baseballs. Pitching with so few balls made it easier to throw a ball with movement. By the sixth inning the ball would be roughed up, which made it move as the rough spots would catch in the air and make the ball dance. All pitchers like to throw a ball that has something on it. Pitchers throwing spitballs made it difficult for their opposing pitcher's control because of the saliva on the ball. And pitchers used to chew tobacco just to have more access to saliva.

Being a pitcher for many years helped me become a better hitter. I would watch a pitcher to find out what his best pitch was so that when I faced him I knew what to look forward to. A pitcher will always go to his best pitch when he needs to throw a strike, and if you know what that is, you can wait on it.

Doctoring bats was a part of baseball just as spitball pitchers were. Some bats were prepared in such a way that it was very hard to detect any illegalities. There were bats that were fixed so well that you had to have a keen eye to catch it. Broken bats were fixed with nails and tape, and often would get by the home plate umpire because they were done so well. If a player had a hot bat that he was hitting well with, he would go to any lengths to protect it. He would keep it in his possession at all times and treasure it. A baseball player in the Negro Leagues during the 1930s and 1940s didn't have an unlimited number of bats at his disposal, so you can believe if he found a piece of wood that favored him, he was going to protect it with all his might.

We had a favorite city where we bought bats. I have spent as much as two hours in stores—which didn't have air-conditioning—just to select a good piece of wood. But, then again, it was my livelihood so it was necessary. To have a favorite bat taken was a heartbreaking experience. As for gloves, they were like a precious baby that had to be watched all the time. What a feeling it was to shape a glove until it fit so well that you adored it. It was like putting on a perfectly fit suit.

Injuries were a part of the game that had to be dealt with. I was fortunate to play for Homestead and never suffer a major injury. Minor injuries didn't stop me; besides, no one was interested in your injuries. It wasn't as if we had medical facilities to treat injuries.

Ballplayers in my time would often rub each other's arms and shoulders. The clubhouse smelled like a hospital because of all the ointments that we applied to each other. But some of these medications lasted only a short time. Once the painkiller's effectiveness wore off, usually around the fifth inning, the rest of the game became a struggle. Hot water gave me more relief from pain than any medication ever did. And once the ointments soaked into your sweaty uniform, the smell would be with you the rest of the road trip. Unless you had an extra sweatshirt you could change into. But this hardly ever happened because if you had an extra shirt, you probably had lent it to someone else.

I see the injuries that sideline players nowadays, and compare them with the Negro League era, and I can't imagine a black player back then missing games for some of the reasons they do today. Being in shape meant everything to me as an athlete, and when an athlete is in shape, things come naturally. So, obviously, I put a great deal of effort into trying to improve my conditioning, I was never satisfied and always believed there was room for improvement.

10

Better Late than Never

Some people didn't know that the Negro Leagues existed before Jackie Robinson signed with the Brooklyn Dodgers in 1946. His signing startled the sports world, and it was a move made by Branch Rickey which contributed to opportunities never before opened to black athletes.

Jackie's teammates told me about the abuse and ridicule that he withstood, and yet he was still able to go out on the field and produce magnificently. He paved the way for future black ballplayers with his conduct and his talent. He carried himself in such a way that he was a role model for the sports world to follow. If Jackie's skills as a ballplayer had been average, I doubt if he could have taken the many insults that he was showered with. Amazingly, he was able to accept his success on the field without showing anger at his mistreatment off the field. All because of the color of his skin.

Jackie was in a league by himself. Anyone can be a follower, but to be a leader in an area as sensitively charged as segregation is something else. His contributions to the opening of baseball cannot be measured in words, but one has to look around and see the results that followed to truly appreciate the deed. I doubt that I could have endured the hardships that Jackie experienced while he broke into the major leagues—he was truly one-of-a-kind.

Certain conditions prompted Mr. Rickey to venture into the uncharted waters of integration: World War II had opened the eyes of the public when looking at Major League Baseball. They saw that in order for it to survive and be financially successful, changes had to be made. Baseball owners saw up to 20,000 fans streaming into major league parks to see black baseball games, and compared that to some of their own games drawing crowds only half that size, and they realized they would have to acquire black players. Simple as one plus one equals two. Mr. Rickey's move opened the doors for black players, and it influenced other organizations to follow suit or be left behind. This upgraded the value of the sport and, as a result, fans became interested. As fans became interested, financial success was ensured, and the sport once again began to flourish. When President Eisenhower sent a telegram to the club I played on when we won the Global World Series in 1955, it showed just how important the game had become internationally.

Jackie Robinson, in my opinion, is the best-ever black baseball player in the world, not so much for his play, but for his outstanding play in the face of the harrassment and racial discrimination he took on. Not that Jackie was the only black baseball player who ever encountered racism, mind you, but it was the never-ending amount that he took that is mind-boggling. I found that it was better to ignore racism because to confront it would only make things worse. When I played with the Grays, no matter where we had a game, racism was always present. The only difference was that some places and their people were more outspoken and openly racist than others. I could deal with the boos and harrassment to a certain degree, but it was difficult, especially if it involved spectators expressing negative comments about me personally or my loved ones. At times like that my thoughts would become disorganized, and sometimes I would stare in the direction that the comments were coming from.

When we would enter a playing field in the South we would see chicken wire separating the box seats (for white people) and the bleachers (for black people). This occurred even though there would be more black spectators in the bleachers than whites in the box seats. It made me feel like the black fans were being mistreated. But we had a job to do so we had to collect ourselves and put our thoughts of segregation aside in order to concentrate on what we were there for: to win ballgames.

One year during spring training with Toronto, I asked the clubhouse attendant to get me a chair. Now, in the Negro Leagues we called each other nicknames, so I called the clubhouse attendant "horse." He resented me calling him that although I meant him no disrespect. So he got up and left the clubhouse. I went on with what I was doing, and when I had finished suiting up, I went outside. There sat the attendant on the hood of his Model T Ford, and he had a shotgun in his hands. I kept walking toward the field when all of the sudden he fired a shot that knocked a blackbird off of a telephone wire above me. The bird fell in front of me, but I kept right on walking and never said anything to anybody. This was the type of thing we had to go through.

Black baseball died with the integration of the major leagues, and most of the top black players were pursued to play there. And most of them not only succeeded but went on to become stars. This is testimony to the caliber of baseball that was played in the Negro Leagues during its heyday. Only recently has that fact begun to be recognized.

In the last few years black ballplayers from the Negro League-era have begun to receive publicity, which is good because their contribution to American society has been long overlooked. The only black ballplayers most people remember are those who were young enough to move into the majors after integration. Largely forgotten are the black players who played too early to have had a chance at the major leagues, or who chose not to play there for whatever reasons, such as financial considerations (as in my case). And it is only a matter of time before the information and knowledge about these players is lost entirely. That is why it is so important to keep black baseball alive by spreading the word. Many of the older players have died. I am one of the youngest black ballplayers still alive, and I am almost 70 years old.

Fortunately, some recent efforts have been undertaken that have begun to resurrect the memories and histories of the Negro Leagues and its players. The Hall of Fame in Cooperstown, New York, requested and obtained information on the Negro Leagues. Only a few of us were selected and I was fortunate to be one of them. I visited the Hall of Fame with my family, and we had the privilege to see this material there. It was a good feeling.

In June 1989, the Southern Bell Company in conjunction with the Atlanta Braves sponsored a reunion of 81 black baseball players from the Negro Leagues of the 1930s and 1940s. They named us the "Black Legends of Baseball." We even got to bring our wives. It was truly a class act.

To meet with ballplayers that I hadn't seen in 40 years was a breathtaking experience. It seemed as though it was only a short while ago that we had played together or against each other. We stared at each other as if to say: "Is this really happening?" We reminisced for three days and nights. I will remember those three days forever.

For those players who were unable to attend because of illness, my prayers go out to them, and I hope that a future reunion will find them present. For the many "Black Legends" who have passed, may their role in the Negro Leagues and their special contributions be remembered. It was very difficult to depart from a fellow "Black Legend" when the reunion ended and it came time to leave Atlanta. Because of our ages we realized it may be the last time many of us would see each other. You could see it in our faces. Maybe there will be another company, or maybe the major leagues will sponsor another reunion. To Southern Bell of Atlanta and the Braves, a special thanks for making the reunion possible and a complete success. It meant so much to all of us.

It felt good to hear some of the ballplayers talk about each other at the reunion. Sam Hairston, a former teammate of mine in Puerto Rico and a manager in the Chicago White Sox organization, said: "Chinky was a player that could do it all." That was nice of him to say. Then there was Bob Thurman, who played with the Grays before joining the Cincinnati Reds as a player. He said: "They used to give you the ball every night, Chinky, especially when we won the World Championship in '48." It's a good feeling to know that someone still remembers you.

Hank Aaron, Don Newcombe, and Ernie Banks all spoke to the "Black Legends" at the reception for us, and they told the truth when they spoke of the value that black ballplayers added to the national pastime. To be a part of this history makes one feel that our accomplishments will not be forgotten. Knowing that I was a part of the black people's movement to improve our status in this work makes my life more comfortable. Hank Aaron said that he'd have never had the opportunity to hit 755 home runs and set the all-time record if it hadn't been for the "Black Legends" who preceded him. After all, he pointed out, he started his baseball career in the Negro Leagues.

Recently 15 Black Legends of Baseball were invited by the Philadelphia Phillies' organization and Upper Deck Sports to Philadelphia. Our accommodations and treatment were good as usual. Joe Black, a former Brooklyn Dodgers' pitcher, treated us unbelievably well. And we had another surprise. Lou Brock, the former St. Louis Cardinal who set many records including breaking the 3,000 hit barrier, spoke to us. Talking about the old times and laughing continuously filled our time there. We attended a ballgame between the Phillies and the Montreal Expos. They also had a Phillies' Old-Timers Game and we were able to meet with some of the old Phillies' players, such as Jim Bunning, Rusty Staub, Rick Wise, and others. I met the Phillies owner,

Bill Giles, and Bill White, an all-star major leaguer who is currently the President of the National League. After the reception we were introduced to the crowd out on the playing field.

During our announcement to the fans, the public address announcer gave some history on each player as well as their achievements. The fans gave us a great reception. It was good to hear 40,000 people cheer you instead of boos! They had a flag raised in centerfield with the Negro League's name on it, and that tells me we'll be remembered. My wife and I really enjoyed the occasion and we were grateful to the Phillies for inviting and honoring us.

I have worked to keep the history of black baseball alive, and am involved with the Negro League Justice Association (NLJA). This is an organization that works to keep black baseball alive. At a recent conference in Baltimore, Maryland, we discussed the contributions that black baseball players made to baseball, and we tried to decide ways to not only keep black baseball in the public's awareness, but ways to help out some of our older members who may be struggling financially. We proposed autograph sessions to benefit those in need; that is something that is in great demand from the public. A problem with an organization of this type is that the people who are trying to work with us to keep black baseball alive are at a handicap. So few records and so little information has been kept over the years that only a few people have any real and comprehensive knowledge of the reality of that world. I am lucky because my wife kept probably 95 percent of the news clippings and records of my performances. So this is one of the reasons I am writing this book—to pass on the history of black baseball.

At the "Black Legends" weekend sponsored by the Phillies, I spoke with Lou Brock for several hours about marketing strategies for black ballplayers. Brock is experienced in this kind of endeavor, so it was interesting to listen to him explain in detail his plans to help the Black Legends of Baseball. I stay busy trying to contact former owners of black ballclubs and their family members to get permission to use the clubs' logos while we promote memorabilia. There are several organizations that are promoting our movement. After 40 years, the recognition we are receiving has brought us from out of the dark. The players in the Negro Leagues from the 1930s and 1940s are now getting their overdue recognition. We feel that most everyone will cooperate in helping us accomplish our forgotten dream. But we must hurry. Many of us have already passed away, and time is working against us. There are so many obstacles to overcome because it has been 41 years since the Negro Leagues went out of existence.

At the NLJA meeting in Baltimore, I met with a representative from the museum of Black Baseball which is based in Kansas City, and he filled me in on its plans for a museum there that will contain the Black Baseball Hall of Fame. Although this endeavor is long overdue, it is better late than never.

We are hoping the recent interest in black baseball history will continue because there is still so much to be learned about the era. But we're making good progress, as demonstrated by the turnout at the NLJA meeting. There were players from all over, including California and Mexico.

These meetings always bring out the baseball card collectors. These collectors always amaze me because they have some of my baseball cards and pictures from as far back as the 1940s. It's nice to be recognized for your contributions and to feel they still mean something.

In carrying the black baseball message, I try to make as many speaking engagements as possible. But sometimes it's almost impossible to fulfill all of the requests. I've had as many as three requests per week. I wish I was able to furnish all the information that people wanted about black baseball players.

One morning I got up at 3:30 a.m. and tried to answer as many letters as I could before work. By 6:30 a.m. I was tired. I try to do this because there are very few black baseball players left, so the amount of information that can be put out is limited. That's another reason I'm writing this book: to reach as many people as fast as possible.

I speak at schools, churches, and different organizations in the attempt to carry the black-baseball banner. It is gratifying to receive mail from people all over the U.S. and Canada who want to know about the Homestead Grays or black baseball in general. I am more than happy to accommodate them in any way I can.

Recently, I received a letter from an attorney in New Jersey who wanted to acquire any memorabilia that I had. Then there was a professor from Chicago who wanted the statistics and records that I had collected of myself. A journalist from New York is trying to sell some of the material that he acquired from me. Certain people want certain items and the demand is high.

Some journalists are doing a good job of helping to keep black baseball alive. John Holway, a good friend of mine and the author of *Black Diamonds*, has done a wonderful job, as have others, of capturing the essence of black baseball. On the cover of *Black Diamonds* is my picture along with Dave Barnhill and Max Manning. It is a real honor to be included with such players.

A representative from a company in California that presents programs on CBS television called me and asked if they could interview me for a program. The show was titled "The Other Side of Victory," and when it is shown on CBS I hope everyone will see it because it tells the truth about black baseball.

A Colorado man contacted me not too long ago and shared some inspiring hopes regarding black baseball. He is trying to establish a place that could be used for another reunion of Negro League players. He also wants to create an Old-Timer's Game to be played in a major league park. What a tremendous affair that would be. All of these efforts are encouraging and I hope they will continue.

As nice as the attention and efforts to promote black baseball are, nothing compares with the feelings that arise when black players get a chance to reunite and share their past together. I visited a former teammate of mine, Walter "Buck" Leonard, down in North Carolina a few years ago, and it was one of the most moving experiences I've ever had.

We talked about his days of playing, which began in 1924 (when I was two years old), and we went through the end of my career, which came in 1958. He was twice my age when I played ball with him. We talked about the good times and the bad, we talked about how it seemed that black baseball players played for the love of the game rather than for money, and we talked about some of the people and memories of them that we shared.

I have never enjoyed a conversation so much. We sat in his den and talked about almost everything, and we agreed on almost everything, too. We did this for about three hours until I noticed he was getting tired. After all, he was 83 years old at the time, and had suffered a stroke. I embraced him and told him I would see him later. When I went out the door he tried to follow me. He was and still is a warrior. I had to embrace him again. He was one of the main reasons my life in baseball turned out as it did. He was the one who gave me and our first son the name of "Chinky." It was good to see his wife, a dedicated lady, take such good care of him. After I left his house with my wife, I was overcome with a deep feeling of emotion. My wife asked me what was the matter and I told her I was just feeling the impact of my memories with Buck—they will always be a part of me. I hope I see him again.

Someone calls me every day wanting to talk about black baseball. An old-timer called me and talked for a half-hour. He talked about his entire career. I think he wanted to be heard. I wasn't able to say much because he never stopped talking, but we did discover that we had a couple things in common. We both remembered playing at 44th Street and Parkside in Philadelphia. That ballpark is so memorable because it was the worst I ever played in. Smoke would fill the stadium when a train passed by, and we would have to stop the game when it got too bad. The combination of smoke and a dim set of lights made my fastball faster. So, I would hurry my delivery when the smoke was in the air!

One of the obstacles that confronted me as a child was the unavailability of news about black baseball and its players. That's another reason why my desire is so strong to pass on the information about black baseball. No one but my wife, Audrey, knows all of my baseball history, but I'm trying to share as much as possible via this book. My feelings about black baseball only strengthen over the years because of what it meant to the progress of the black race, and what it can mean in the future to all black people. The strength of black baseball has greatly increased during the last three years. If someone asked me today if I regretted not accepting a major league contract, I would have to say no—although the money sure is tempting—because I was meant to have a career in the Negro Leagues. While it is the desire of most ballplayers to play in the major leagues because it says, "I am a success—I play against the best," it was never my desire. When I was young I prayed that God would give me the ability to play black baseball, and for that gift I am most grateful. I also got to play against major leaguers in Latin American countries and Canada, so I never doubted if I could play with them because I did, and quite well, in fact.

11
Everything Starts with Family

It's hard for any ballplayer to adjust his baseball lifestyle to an even keel with his family lifestyle. Because of a sometimes grueling baseball schedule—especially when I was with the Grays—it was hard to maintain a regular family lifestyle. But because the home fields of the Grays were in Pittsburgh and Washington, D.C., I was able to see my family more than would have otherwise been possible. My marriage to Audrey—45 years strong—has been an uplifting one. Being a black professional athlete in the 1940s and 1950s meant dealing with trials and tribulations every day of your life. But the faith that Audrey and I have shared throughout our lives has carried us and made our lives enjoyable ones. It would have been a difficult task to go through life without faith.

My mother and father believed that love in a family was the cure for all ailments. Therefore, religion and love played all-important parts in our lives.

My mother was a hard-working woman who believed that her children needed loving care at all times. She was always trying to find ways to improve the living conditions of her family. Her school education was limited, but her knowledge of the important values in life was great. She found ways to make ends meet although we didn't have much money. Her pies, cakes, and good country cooking made life a welcome dream. Our clothes were few, but they were always clean. She never turned away anyone in need, and always fed the hungry. She left a legacy of love that shines today in both her children and grandchildren.

My father worked 33 years at a lumber yard, and he was the hardest working man you'd ever want to meet. We had a small farm where he raised animals, fruits, and vegetables. He supplied his family with plenty of food. His personal expenses were almost none. Mom would buy him a couple of boxes of Prince Albert smoking tobacco and a piece of Mule Chewing Tobacco every weekend, and he'd keep 50 cents in his pocket for a soft drink. A new pair of overalls and a couple of blue handkerchiefs every Christmas were the extent of his personal expenses. He would put shoes on his horses before he'd put them on himself. I will never forget all the vegetables and fruits he would bring in the house. We'd have enough canned in the cellar to carry us through the winter, and usually have some left over. Dad would also make grape and cherry wines for his friends. He would do odd jobs for people as well. He worked from sun-up until sun-down, and he was the hardest working, most unselfish man I've ever known.

A memory of him that I'll always cherish was when the town baseball team asked my father and me to play with them. He was 40 and I was 10. I played second base and he played the outfield. He hit a double between the other team's outfielders. This is an everlasting memory.

Our family thanks God for giving us the parents He did.

My oldest brother Morris—whom everyone called "Moogie"—never got angry that I can recall. He was always able to adjust to even the most difficult situations. His love for baseball, football, and fishing rubbed off on me and played a big part in my life. He possessed the rare ability to get along with everyone. Because our careers took us in different directions, we weren't able to be around each other very much, but his qualities as a human being still stand as a model for the present and future generations.

My second oldest brother, Marvin, was a determined person who believed in the good qualities of life. He got his Doctorate Degree in Science from Ohio State University, and then he went on to teach for 45 years—mostly at Virginia State College. Marvin loved sports and played baseball and football. He stayed involved in sports in some capacity or another throughout his entire teaching career. He worked all the time to try and improve and provide his family with life's necessities. His contributions to his family were honorable and it was always his first priority. Whenever one of us needed help he was always there. Right up through his last days with us he tried to impress on us the importance of the values of life.

My third brother, Oliver, worked his whole life, and, in fact, is still working today at the age of 72. He has enjoyed all sports, and played several of them. I will never forget the time he made three touchdowns against a strong Douglas High School team from Baltimore. He had the ability to be even better at baseball than he was in football, but he never gave himself the chance. We live about 100 yards apart and we see each other frequently. When we were boys we had a lot of fun and created a lot of fond memories through our sports involvement. He looked after me in a manner that only can be described as loving.

My sister Evelyn was the one who always got her way. She used to enjoy playing baseball with us, but was unable to play for her high school softball team because it didn't exist! She would have made an outstanding ballplayer. She excelled in school and finished second in her high school graduating class. She went to Virginia Union University, and then earned her Master's Degree from a school in New York before coming back to Manassas and teaching for 42 years. She is the superintendent of the Sunday school and a committed member of the church. She is constantly contributing to the community and is a dedicated human being. In the final days of my parents, her love stood out like a lit up Christmas tree. She was our only sister and she still looks for, and receives, our eternal brotherly love. She, too, lives very close to me—only 40 yards away—and we visit frequently.

My mother and father, Mabel and Albert Fields, and my brothers, Morris and Marvin (all deceased), left me with something special. Something that individuals can't accomplish on their own in life. They gave me a wonderful life; the roles they played and the way they helped shape me as I matured is an everlasting gift that gives me a feeling of security.

I think about the hardships they endured to establish a stable life, and I give thanks every day for parents and brothers that the Lord gave us. They will be a part of my life forever.

I married Audrey in 1946, in Gretna, Louisiana. We never had a honeymoon, but I hope that I've made up for that over the years. We have been very fortunate to travel many places together, and we have met many wonderful people around the world. Because my wife is from the South, she is a very friendly person who has always been surrounded with friends. Religion has played a big part in our marriage; in fact, our daily duties require that God be involved in everything we say or do. After my baseball career, Audrey went to work for two doctors: Dr. Hahn and Dr. Cole. She is a hard-working mother, and she still looks after her children even though her youngest one is 30 years old!

We all live close together and she sees her children and grandchildren every day. Audrey is a dedicated person who is always there when someone needs her. Her contribution to our family is one of the reasons that love has played such an important part in our successful marriage. When the "Black Legends" were honored in Atlanta, the master of ceremonies had all the wives of the players stand up and be recognized. This was a great and appropriate honor because without our wives' contributions, our baseball careers would have been much more difficult and unpleasant.

To sum up what Audrey has meant to me in a few sentences is not possible. She is a model for others and is as caring and loving today as the day I met her. She was by my side throughout a 25-year baseball career. The Lord has blessed us in so many ways.

We had three children—two boys and a girl. Our children brought out a strong feeling of love in our family.

Our first child was born in 1946 and his name is Marvin Preston after his uncle. His nickname, the one he got from "Buck" Leonard, is "Chinky." Marvin is well-liked and easy to get along with. His love of family and his caring for others are his greatest attributes. We were lucky he survived a dangerous disease called nephritis that he got when he was 11 years old. It sidelined him from doing recreational activities and it effected his kidneys. Despite his bout with this illness, Marvin was later able to receive a football/baseball scholarship to Delaware State University. He married Loretta and they have three children, Michelle, Mark, and Kevin.

Our second child is named Maridel Verone Bates. She was an outstanding high school student and just missed being valedictorian. She married James Bates and their marriage has been a good one. She attended James Madison University and now works for the county government. Maridel and James have been blessed with a daughter named Renee. Maridel is intelligent and determined—she is a fine person who can be trusted, and is a good organizer for her family.

Our third child is Wilmer Leon Fields, Jr., and his nickname is "Billy." He was born on Christmas Day, 1959, and he has made our life enjoyable ever since. He played several sports in high school before going to Providence College on a four-year basketball scholarship. He graduated with a B.S. in History.

The Lord has been good to us and has blessed us in so many ways. We try to instill in our children that faith, love, and communication are the foundations that build a good life.

When your children get old enough to have homes of their own, it often means that their visits decrease. But we are blessed; we see our children every day, and our grandchildren often. Maintaining our close relationship with our children is a custom that was taught to us by our parents. We have our share of problems, but with faith, difficult situations are easier to handle. We sit down with our children and talk about the things that affect our lives. Because of our age difference, it is good to talk with them and learn about things we are unaware of. As parents, we are very surprised to hear about the things that we don't know about. Society has placed a burden on the shoulders of today's parents, in that life these days can be a frightening experience. Our children are determined to maintain a relationship with us and this shows us that their roots have not been forgotten. It is a good feeling to know that your children want to be around you. These days a Mom and Dad mean so much.

We have four grandchildren and two great grandchildren. Our granddaughter Michelle is 22 years old and the mother of one of our great grandchildren. She is an appreciative, understanding, and intelligent person. Michelle is always ready to help others, and is dedicated to her family and loved ones. She is married to Tony Dallas.

Our second granddaughter is Renee. Renee is a true leader and a determined one at that. She is a student at James Madison University, and there are no limits to her future. Renee is married to Mark Ross.

Mark, our third grandchild, believes every day is one for excitement and adventure. He has the potential to become a well-respected person once he realizes the facts of life, and the sacrifices that go along with them.

Kevin is our fourth grandchild. He is 16 years old and is 6-foot-4, 200 pounds. I would say he can go as far in life as he desires. He was having trouble in school but has the potential to be a good student. He has begun to realize that his other achievements mean very little without an education and he has begun to improve. Kevin plays on his high school basketball team, and he is quick and well-coordinated for his size.

Brandon is one of our great grandchildren and he is a bundle of joy. He loves attention. I can't wait for the day that he comes to the house by himself.

We are very fortunate to have our children and their families live within visiting distance. Once again, the Lord has truly blessed us.

12
Looking Back

I have one regret in life: I wish my parents and brothers could have seen this book published and had the opportunity to enjoy some of the recognition that the "Black Legends" of baseball have received during the past few years.

As a young boy, the thought of segregation never interfered with the happy days I enjoyed so much with my family, and our friends. But as I grew older and saw the areas of life I had been deprived of because I was black, I felt left out. A question that constantly ran through my mind was: "Is this the way a black person in a small town only 30 miles from the nation's capital is supposed to live?" It would have been so much better if I would have had the chance to prove myself.

We tried hard to improve our academic skills as students, and I can't recall any students repeating a school year in my high school. I'm not saying we were perfect students, but our idea of life was a positive one and we pointed to the future.

I would have liked to have had the opportunity to play golf with a golf club rather than a piece of iron rod; to have played tennis with a racket instead of a board; to have played basketball in a gymnasium instead of against the side of a barn. But my life has been so filled with the goodness of family and friends that it has been a blessing.

Then the opportunity came for me to leave home and play for the Grays. I wasn't the first country black ballplayer to leave home and get involved with a completely different type of society. Nevertheless, this society proved difficult to deal with. As a result, I had to adjust so that my future would be beneficial. Thankfully, my parents prepared me with the power of faith which enabled me to endure those hard days. I learned to deal with city life by keeping my mouth shut and taking advantage of what other players said and did. Knowledge didn't come overnight, but it came slowly and steadily with the passage of time. Continuous effort to learn brought out the best of me in my professional life, which I needed because black ballplayers needed more than raw talent back then. Unless you experienced those conditions, you'll never know what it was like. Please don't compare the adjustments that black players had to make back then with the black players of today.

Nothing in my life could have happened as it did without prayer and the Lord. As a young boy in grade school, I would wonder how praying affected the life of a human being, and I decided to pray for some things I wanted to have. Before I became a teenager I prayed for a career in professional baseball, even though there were no blacks in organized baseball at the time. As I grew older I learned about black professional baseball and my prayers became more earnest than ever. My desire and determination became more serious too.

During my childhood, certain things happened in my life that made me believe that anything is possible. And this belief has played a crucial role in my life.

I remember one day when I was a child, my brother Morris was working with my uncle building log cabins on a lake. At lunch time, my brother decided he'd wade in the lake. It was a real hot summer day. When Morris went into the water, his feet slipped from under him and he found himself in 10 feet of water unable to swim. My uncle was eating lunch and thought my brother was playing because he came up three times. Then he realized Morris was helpless, so he got a rake as my brother was going down for the last time. My uncle put the rake into the water where Morris had gone down, and Morris grabbed the rake from under the water. My uncle said, "I think I can feel something." So he pulled the rake up and brought Morris up with it. He was holding onto it for dear life!

Not long after that incident, another occurred that was somewhat similar. Again, it was a hot summer day. Two of my cousins, ages 13 and 16, decided to go fishing with four of their friends. They weren't catching any fish, so they climbed into a boat that was docked nearby. They, too, were in 10 feet of water when the boat capsized. My two cousins swam to shore as did two of their friends. But the other two friends couldn't swim, and they went under. The four young men on land tried to decide what to do to save their friends, but no one volunteered to go in after them.

Since no one volunteered, the youngest cousin, Warren Wells, who was the smallest of them, and his brother decided to make a daring attempt to rescue their friends. They quickly got in the boat over the spot where their friends had gone down. Warren went into the water holding one end of a stick, while his older brother sat in the boat holding the other end. While Warren was searching the bottom, he felt someone grab his leg. My older cousin, Paul, felt something very heavy pull on the stick while rowing to shore. Soon Warren and the two friends who were drowning became visible. That was when the two young men on land helped them to shore. The two young men that were drowning were clutching each other. Without the courageous rescue by Warren and Paul, their friends would certainly have drowned. These incidents strengthened my faith and I know God is everywhere.

My prayers for a career in baseball were answered as you have read—the Lord was with me all the time. He guides me through each day, and without Him I would have never seen my dream come true. Regardless of the circumstances and conditions that have existed during my life, the Lord always has made a way for me to overcome the hard times.

These last few years have made all the hardships worthwhile. As a member of the "Black Legends of Baseball," I feel obligated to provide the public with the information needed to keep black baseball alive.

In closing, I would like to say, it has been a privilege to express the facts of life about black baseball players in the 1930s, 1940s, and 1950s. The Lord has made a way for this to happen—showing people that love for black baseball was very strong. Other black players have also made some evaluations of their careers. It has been a real thrill to relive my past life—to remember people and places that might have been forgotten if I hadn't written this book.

I remember a friend of mine, Satchel Paige, saying, "don't look back, someone might be gaining on you." This is one time I looked back and gained enough inspiration to help write this autobiography. This book has given me a feeling of relief. If we as black baseball players don't express our feelings about our careers, no one will ever know the true facts of our lives.

It is very hard to forget these days of struggle. People shake their heads and stare at me when I try to explain to them the life of a black in the days before and after Jackie Robinson's rise to the majors. Sometimes I find myself reminiscing about my past for 10 or 15 minutes. These memories will live with me. Again the Lord has made a way for all of this to happen for me. May God bless all of you.

Appendix

The following is a list of many key individuals of the Negro National and American Leagues that made them strong organizations:

Negro National League

Homestead Grays
Josh Gibson
Walter "Buck" Leonard
Sam Bankhead
Ray Brown
Roy Partlow
Garnet Blair
Luke Easter
Eudie Napier
Bill Pope
Lick Carlisle
Jelly Jackson
B. Wilson
Luis Marquez
Rabroy Gaston
Jerry Benjamin
Bob Thurman
Roy Welmaker

Newark Eagles
Monte Irvin
Lenny Pearson
Max Manning
Rufus Lewis
Jimmy Hill
Johnny Davis
Larry Doby
Biz Makey

Philadelphia Stars
Barney Brown
"Red" Parnell
P. Woods
Bill Cash
Gene Benson

Baltimore Elite Giants
Willy Wills
Bill Byudi
Al Bambrey
Jim Gilliam
Joe Black
Tubby Scales
Felton Snow
Pee Wee Butts
Larry Kimbro
Lester Lockett
Leon Day

New York Cubans
Dave Barnhill
Barney Morris
Minnie Minoso
Luis Tiant
A. Crepeo
H. Rodrigues
Lou Louden

Negro National League, cont.

New York Black Yankees
Bud Barbue
Nick Stanley
Buster Haywood
T. Barber

American Negro League

Cleveland Buckeyes
Quincy Trouppe
Sam Jethroe
Al Smith
Chet Brewer

Birmingham Black.Barons
Alonzo Perry
Piper Davis
Artie Wilson

Memphis Red Sox
Dan Bankhead

Chicago American Giants
J. Jessup
"Double Duty" Radcliffe

Kansas City Monarchs
Willard Brown
Hank Thompson
Satchel Paige
Connie Johnson
Hilton Smith
Buck O'Neil
Jim Lemarque
Earl Taborn

Indianapolis Clowns
Sam Hairston

Wilmer Fields Statistics

United States				Venezuela****			
*Homestead Grays**	W	L		1951–52	.392		
1939	2	1		1952–53	.350, MVP		
1940	13	4		1950	.360		
1941	9	3					
1942	14	2		*Colombia*			
1943 (in service)				1955–56	.319		
1944 (in service)				1956–57	.328, MVP		
1945 (in service)							
1946	16	1		*Dominican*		W	L
1947	14	6		*Republic*			
1948	15	3		1953	.397	5	5
1949	12	1					
1950	9	0		*Panama*			
Total	104	21		1949	.360		
*Ft. Wayne***				*Cuba*			
1956	.432, MVP	4	1	1948	.340		
1957	.400	5	2				
				Mexico			
St. Joe				1958	.398		
1949	.397	2	1				
				Canada		W	L
Latin America				1951	.381, MVP	9	1
San Juan		W	L	1952	.299		
1947–48	.328	5	5	1953	.379, MVP	8	2
				1954	.425, MVP	6	1
*Mayagüez****							
1948–49	.332, MVP	9	3				
1949–50	.331	8	2				
1950–51	.338	5	2				

*Homestead Grays won eight pennants from 1939–1950.
**Won National and Global World Series in 1956 with Ft. Wayne. Received congratulations from President Eisenhower.
***Mayagüez, P.R. won pennant in 1948–49.
****Caracas, Venezuela ballclub won pennant in 1952–53.

Index

Aaron, Hank 70
Aparicio, Luis 41
Arlington, Va. 31
Atlanta Black Crackers 10
Atlanta Braves 69, 70
Atlanta, Ga. 25, 70, 78

Ballston, Va. 3
Baltimore Elite Giants ix, 18, 22, 62
Baltimore, Md. 71, 72
Bankhead, Dan 36
Bankhead, Sam 9, 11, 20, 22, 23, 24, 26, 61
Banks, Ernie 70
Barnes, Rev. 7
Barnhill, Dave 73
Baseball Hall of Fame 69
Bates, Maridel Verone 78
Beaver Falls, Pa. 23
Benjamin, Jerry 22
Birmingham Black Barons xi, 20, 25
Black Diamonds 73
Black, Joe 70
Blair, Garnet x–xi, 10
Brantford, Ont. 40, 42, 44
Brock, Lou 70, 71
Brooklyn Dodgers xi, 10, 11, 31, 67, 70
Brown, Ray 10, 62
Brown, Willard 64
Brunswick, N.Y. 10
Buffalo, N.Y. 12, 22, 43
Bunning, Jim 70
Burdette, Lou x
Butts, Tom "Pee Wee" ix, 62

Camp Plachea, La. 27, 30
Canadian Baseball 39–44
Caracas, Venezuela 36, 41, 42
Cardiff, Wales 27
Carlisle, Leonard "Lick" 12–13, 22

Carrasquel, Chico 41
Chicago White Sox 41, 70
Cincinnati Reds xi, 70
Cleveland Buckeyes 19
Cleveland Indians xi, 64
Conners, Chuck 36
Cooke, Jack Kent 36, 42, 43
Cooperstown, N.Y. 69

Danville, Va. 25
Detroit Tigers 11
Doby, Larry x, 64
Dressen, Charlie 31

Easter, Luke xi, 22
Easterling, Howard 22
Eisenhower, Dwight D. 68

Fairfax, Va. 3
Fields, Albert 1, 75–76, 77
Fields, Audrey ix, 30, 31, 33, 41, 42, 74, 75, 77, 78
Fields, Billy ix
Fields, Evelyn 1, 31, 77
Fields, Mabel 1, 75, 77
Fields, Marvin Preston "Chinky" 1, 40, 76, 77, 78
Fields, Morris 1, 76, 77, 82
Fields, Oliver 1, 2, 76
Fields, Wilmer Leon, Jr. 78
Forbes Field 18
Fort Meade, Md. 30
Fort Wayne, Ind. 59

Gaston, "Rabroy" 22
Gehrig, Lou 2
Gibson, Josh ix, x, 19, 20, 22, 23
Giles, Bill 71
Gomez, Lefty 2
Gretna, La. 77
Griffith Stadium 2, 10, 12, 14, 18

Hairston, Sam 70

Harris, Vic x, xi, 5, 11, 18, 22, 61, 62
Holman, Art 39
Holway, John, 73
Homestead Grays x, xi, 3, 5, 6, 7, 9–26, 32, 35, 61, 62, 65, 68, 70, 72, 75, 81
Homestead, Pa. 9, 22

Indianapolis Clowns 12
International League 43
Irvin, Monte 32

Jackson, Jelly 22
Jackson, "Sonny Man" 9
Jethroe, Sammy 19

King, Mike 39

Latin American baseball 32–37
Larton, Les x
Le Havre, France 28
Leonard, Buck ix, 9, 19, 20, 23, 26, 73, 74, 78
Lewis, Lawrence 7
Liverpool, U.K. 27

Manassas Industrial School 7
Manassas, Va. ix, 1, 2, 3, 6, 22, 40, 77
Manning, Max 73
Maracaibo, Venezuela 26, 36, 41
Marquez, Luis 22
Marseilles, France 28, 29
Mayagüez Indians 34
Mayagüez, Puerto Rico 26, 33, 34, 35, 36
Mays, Willie xi, xii
Meuller, Ray xi
Mexico City xii
Mexico City Reds 59
Montreal Expos 70
Montreal, Quebec 31

Napier, "Eudie" 22
Negro American League 6, 17, 18
Negro League Justice Association (NLJA) 71, 72
Negro National League 6, 12, 17, 18, 19, 25

Newark Eagles 22
Newark, N.J. x
Newcombe, Don 70
New Orleans, La. xi, 30
New York 11, 27, 33
New York Black Yankees 31
New York Cubans 22
New York Grants x
New York Yankees 2, 11, 31
Nice, France 29
Nokesville, Va. 6

Oakland, Calif. 31

Paige, Satchel ix, x, 83
Partlow, Roy 10
Pearson, Monte 22
Pennell, Lany 39, 40
Philadelphia, Pa. 70
Philadelphia Phillies 70
Pittsburgh 7, 9, 12, 13, 18, 20, 75
Podres, Johnny 43
Pope, Bill 10
Posey, Cum 18

Radcliffe, Ted "Double Duty" x
Richmond, Va. 2, 25
Rickey, Branch 67, 68
Robinson, Brooks x
Robinson, Jackie xi, 67, 68, 83
Ruth, Babe 2

St. Joe, Mich. 59
St. Louis Browns 31
St. Louis Cardinals 70
St. Louis, Mo. 12
San Juan, Puerto Rico 22, 32, 33, 35, 37
San Pedro de Macoris, Dominican Republic 43
The Sky Rocket 9
Southern Bell Company 69, 70
Southern League 10, 25
South Wales, U.K. 28
Staub, Rusty 70

Thompson, "Groundhog" 10
Thrice, Bob 21
Thurman, Bob 22, 70
Tisonia, Mr. 59
Toronto, Ont. 42, 43, 68

Upper Deck Sports 70

Valdez 34
Vander Meer, Johnny xi
Virginia State College 7, 76

Walker, Edsel 10
Walker, R. T. xi, 20
Washington, D.C. 2, 5, 6, 12, 34, 75
Washington *Post* ix
Washington Senators 14, 31, 36, 41

Wells, Warren 82–83
Welmaker, Roy 10, 19
Whatley, Dave 22
White, Bill 71
Williams, Chester 22
Wilson, Boojum 12–13, 22
Winston Salem, N.C. 25
Wise, Rick 70
Wright, Johnny 10

Yankee Stadium 6, 31

Interview with Billy Fields, son of Wilmer Fields, himself a former professional athlete who now works with young basketball players:

What did you learn from your father that helps you be a good mentor to the kids you mentor?

Actually it had a lot to do with more than just sports. It had a lot to do with living your life, like getting good grades, how important family was, and always being prepared. You can never practice enough. I think when I do my camp, a lot of parents come up to me and say, "It's great that you're teaching basketball, but you're also teaching things about life that these kids need to know now." I think those are the biggest things that my father gave to me as far as passing it on.

Did he coach you a lot when you were growing up?

Oh yes, he coached me for ten years in baseball. He really didn't coach me in basketball. It was more of the mental aspect of just being prepared and taking care of your body and just doing the right thing as far as basketball was concerned, but he coached me for baseball for ten years.

What did he tell you about being a member of a team?

Just about to be there when someone having a rough day or to always pick up your teammates, because one day you're going to be there and they're going to pick you up. As I think and look back some of the baseball teams that he coached that I played on, we were all very tight in that group. We were tighter and more connected in how we viewed each other than any other teams we played against. I think that it had a lot to do with our success.

Did you ever see you father play?

When I was born my father retired. The year that I was born, my dad retired. I did see him play in some reunion games, like old timers' games. I did go to Puerto Rico with them and they played, the American Ball Players against the Puerto Rican ball players. It was very entertaining.

At that time, I think my dad was probably in his early 50's. He still had some stuff in him. I mean, you could tell that he had played ball, when he was out pitching or whatever he was doing. Up in Canada, I remember I was sitting on the third baseline and they were playing against the young players up there. I'll never forget my dad hit the home run in the game. When he came by, he certainly, he pointed it out and I'll never forget that, because I was just like, "Wow!"

Your dad mentioned in the beginning of the book that he wanted to explain why he would prefer to play in the Negro Leagues than accept the to offer play in the Major Leagues. Tell me a little bit about what you think that says about him and about why that was important to him.

I think it gave him more opportunity to play different positions. Now, you have your ball players now that if you pitch, you pitch. You don't play in the other positions. Back then, the players got paid more money for playing different positions. I think his potential income was higher playing the way he was playing because he played different positions and he would play in the States in the summer time and get go down and play in Latin America in the winter time. I'm thinking it had a lot to do with the financial situation.

Then again, after I saw him around some of his ex-teammates who played with him in the Negro Leagues, they were very tight, very close. It was actually good to just to see that, take it as a learning experience.

Can you tell me a little bit about what he did to help the people who had been in the Negro Leagues to make sure that they got pensions from Major Leagues baseball?

When my father became the president of the Negro Leagues, I would take him every month over to Baltimore to see a lawyer over there, who was sort of handling the legal stuff that was going on with the Negro Leagues and between the Major Leagues. He was in charge of getting the Negro League ball players' pension from the Major Leagues. I was like, "I don't know if that's going to happen," but it did happen. Then, they also had health insurance from the Major Leagues.

The pension ended after each player had passed away, but the health insurance was passed on to their spouse. For a lot of those ball players, they really didn't have anything. For them to get a pension and to have health benefits for the rest of their life, it was a big thing. I remember answering the phone at the house when I would be home with my parents and the ball players would be calling and thanking him for what he'd done. He really cared a lot about the ball players. He was good. It just wasn't going through the motions.

www.ingramcontent.com/pod-product-compliance
Lightning Source LLC
Chambersburg PA
CBHW060819050426
42449CB00008B/1737